I0520779

ALWAYS
AT CHOICE

Strategies For Moving On After the Death
of a Spouse or Life Trauma

Praise for *Always At Choice*

"As a communication and mindfulness coach, I often work with people facing the fear, uncertainty, and self-doubt that can arise when life doesn't go as planned or hoped. A major turning point comes when someone realizes they do have choice—even around a circumstance they didn't choose. That kind of courage runs alongside a fragile but powerful belief: that there is another possibility. In *Always At Choice*, Larry Freeborg speaks to that very journey. He doesn't shy away from the pain of loss or from the pain we create for ourselves when we're stuck inside beliefs that no longer serve us. I've found that one of the most liberating questions we can ask in difficult moments is: What's possible here? This book helps us begin to explore that."

—Christine D. Trani
Another Possibility LLC

"To have a choice is merely to face options; to be at choice is to inhabit them consciously and freely. Through vivid lessons drawn from his remarkable journey of loss, growth, and redemption, Larry Freeborg invites us to uncover and embody our deepest values and commitments. Who we are emerges not from conforming to norms or dogmas, but from choosing our authentic selves—deliberately and in full awareness. Only by staking ourselves in each moment do we author our own Being. Blending personal wisdom with philosophical and therapeutic insights and resources, and grounding his practical guidance in leading organizational practices, Freeborg offers a rich manual for *re-firing*: the art of reinventing our best selves—at any age and at every stage of life."

—Tomasz R. Okon, MD
Consultant, Division of Palliative Medicine
Mayo Clinic Health System
Assistant Professor of Medicine

"Over the past few years, I've had the privilege of getting to know Larry and benefiting from his insight and wisdom—now I'm thrilled to see him share that with the world through *Always at Choice*. Larry has helped me realize that no matter the circumstances, I am always at choice. I'm responsible for the choices I make, and the assumptions I carry often get in the way of my goals and relationships. That understanding has been transformational, not only in my own life but in the lives of many Larry has influenced throughout his life and career.

In *Always at Choice*, Larry offers readers a powerful and personal invitation into his journey—from heartbreak and loss to healing, clarity, and lifelong learning. His authenticity, humility, and hard-earned perspective challenge us to pause, reflect, and take ownership of our stories. This book will encourage you to view your experiences through a new lens and empower you to move forward with greater awareness, self-compassion, and intention."

—Steph Altom
SJA Coaching

ALWAYS AT CHOICE

Strategies For Moving On After the Death
of a Spouse or Life Trauma

LARRY FREEBORG

Seshat Press
211 Pauline Drive #513
York, PA 17402
www.seshatpress.com
Send questions to: support@seshatpress.com

Paperback ISBN: 979-8-9920502-7-1
eBook ISBN: 979-8-9920502-8-8
Library of Congress Control Number: 2025917760

Cover Design: Ranilo Cabo
Layout: Ranilo Cabo
Editor and Proofreader: Heather Taylor
Book Midwife: Karen Everitt

Printed in the United States of America

Seshat Press is proud to be a part of the Tree Neutral˚ program. Tree Neutral offsets the number of trees consumed in the production and printing of this book by taking proactive steps such as planting trees in direct proportion to the number of trees used to print books. To learn more about Tree Neutral, please visit treeneutral.com.

I dedicate this book to:

The many healthcare professionals who have helped people like me move through the emotions of a significant loss of a loved one and enabled us to positively move forward in our lives.

Dodie Driscoll, the woman who has been the wind beneath my wings and enabled me to soar. Unfortunately, she passed on just before the book was published.

My high school English teacher, Mrs. Margaret Glenn. She challenged and inspired me to read and opened me up to learning in a big way.

All the good work that Equine's and Equine Coaches are doing, helping people move through trauma and tragedy.

Preface

You may think it strange that a Sailing Ship is on the cover of a self-help book for people moving on after the death of a spouse and life trauma, but for me, it has a lot of meaning. Let me explain.

The picture of the sailing ship is from a copper rubbing I made when I was in the psychiatric ward, recovering from the loss of my wife and my job in the middle of an economic downturn. There were many other losses I experienced at the same time, but my main focus was learning how to take care of my four children as a single parent. No wife, no job, no money is where I was starting from.

This ship rubbing became a symbol of recovery for me.

It represents a galleon—a big ship, a symbol of myself—with all the sails up, full of wind, being taken care of by a bunch of sailors with various responsibilities, pulling out of a dark and vicious storm into the sunshine. It represented what I intended to do with my life.

I intended to live fully engaged, capitalizing on the experiences and gifts of many others along the way. I intended to sail in the sunshine, taking care of my kids in the best way I could learn.

I hope reading this book assists you to do the same.

—Larry Freeborg, November 19, 2024

Contents

Introduction

I'm currently eighty-six years old. My life lessons began before I was forty, but at forty, I realized it was necessary and could be extremely valuable to look at the world differently and adopt new beliefs. Two key beliefs I adopted are 1) I'm *always at choice*, and 2) I'm accountable and responsible for what I create in my life.

When I say I'm *always at choice*, I mean that every moment that I'm alive, I'm always in a position to make a choice. The operative word is *at*. Some people will say I always *have* a choice. I've learned that because the choice lives within me, I'm always *at* choice. I may not be able to choose the circumstances I'm in, but I always have a choice regarding how I respond: Do I accept the circumstances beyond my control, or do I convert my thinking and see what the gift and opportunity is? Where do I invest my effort? What do I give my time to?

I am a synthesizer and integrator. In this book, I share the beliefs I have embraced after having tried them and ensuring they work for me. I'd love to say that all the ideas are mine, but they're not. I have incorporated many ideas from my learning journey with many great teachers. I have developed some of the refinements.

Somewhere along my journey, I heard the statement, "Experience is the best teacher, but it doesn't always have to be mine. I can learn from others' experiences." I have integrated this thought and looked for teachers and mentors from whom I could learn.

Live Life More Fully

Not all the lessons came easily. One critical life lesson I learned when I was dealing with the trauma, chaos, and overwhelm of losing my thirty-nine-year-old wife, Shirley, to leukemia and becoming a widower with four young children. The situation got even more complicated when, because of a downturn in the economy, my job was eliminated at a company where I'd worked for more than eighteen years. There I was, with no wife and no money, in the middle of a significant recession when unemployment was between 10 and 12 percent and interest rates were 18–20 percent, learning how to find a new job and raise four kids. I admit I was scared.

In this book, I write about how my life and family worked out. I share the trials I encountered and how I learned to deal with them. I'm happy to report that all four of my children graduated from the colleges of their choice, and we have become a loving, close family. After considerable trial and error, and fifteen years after Shirley's death, I finally created a loving relationship with another life partner I and my children adore.

I became a sought-after strategic planning facilitator and life transformation coach and developed many close, loving friendships and fun life adventures. Within two years of becoming an independent contractor, I created more income than while previously working for Corporate America as an employee.

At eighty-six, I've come up with a couple of questions I've adopted and reflect on regularly:

Life is short—how much time do I have left?
Am I using it wisely?

For years, I've celebrated my accomplishments annually and consciously tracked how I have used my time to determine whether I have been fulfilling my goals and life objectives. This practice has become even more critical at my age. I've had the opportunity to reflect, acknowledge what I've accomplished, and consider the time I have left to accomplish things I'd like to achieve in my life before I pass.

Along the way, I learned an exercise from Life Coach Richard Leider. It's a life spiral that enables me to look at the year I was born, my current age, and my speculation about how long I expect to live.

This spiral gets more expansive as it goes up. The concept is that our options expand because of the depth of our experience as we age. The challenge to this model is that while our options get broader as we age, our capacity to undertake many options diminishes because of our mental and physical health.

At eighty-six, it's registering with me how short life is. At thirty-nine, Shirley died too soon.

According to life expectancy timetables, back in 1935, when Social Security was created, people lived at most sixty or sixty-five years. That's why, in my way of looking at things, I'm currently in what I call *my gifted years*. Any time beyond eighty is my *gifted* time, as I only expected to live to be eighty-four. Now, I've set my goal for ninety-three, if I can be active and productive.

My approach has been to return to what I've chosen to be my purpose in life. My focus has been and continues to be creatively capitalizing on my natural gifts and talents wherever they take me to serve others where my values align.

My commitment is to:

1. Share my learning experiences in this book
2. Improve my public speaking skills and share my beliefs with others

I have struggled to discover ideas that serve me better than those I learned growing up. I intend in this book to share my thoughts and selected beliefs so you may benefit and achieve your life goals with less struggle. I'd be delighted for you to choose some of the ideas I've selected. I hope they help you live a happy and fulfilled life.

The five key metrics for success in my life today are:

1. My wife, Dodie's, health and mine
2. My relationship with Dodie—are we having fun, sharing plenty of laughter and enjoyable experiences?
3. My relationships with my adult children and their families
4. My relationships with my extended family and friends
5. My contribution to others with needs and whether it's meaningful

When I look at my measurements of success, I'm doing well.

It's All About Perspective

This perspective returns to my foundational belief that I'm *always at choice*. Life comes to me, and I choose how I deal with it. When meeting what's been coming my way, I could view certain situations and feel discouraged, sad, down and out, or I could look at the situation as an opportunity, a gift, and speculate what possibilities arise from this experience.

From my perspective, I'm not responsible for the hurricane, snowstorm, flood, or my wife's death, but I am responsible for how I deal with them.

The challenge now is for me to release the dreams I had when I was younger and to investigate what's possible, given my current situation.

Reading this book can help you learn to:

- Live as an active, accountable creator of your life instead of as a victim
- Creatively capitalize on your natural gifts and talents
- Live your life with purpose and serve others meaningfully
- Coordinate action more effectively through language
- Make and manage promises and differentiate opinions and interpretations (assessments) from facts (assertions)
- Declare the life you desire
- Manage your mood and emotions
- Adopt a practice of celebrating blessings daily and sharing them with others
- Learn how to deal with loss and grief and to ask for help

My unique gift is helping individuals overcome the significant losses they have experienced and become fully engaged in new life possibilities. In businesses, I've helped leaders solve major strategic business problems and gain clarity regarding what they'd like to create by using my facilitation skills, the wisdom of the group, and coaching experience.

I hope you find the stories of my learning journey helpful for yours.

Blessings.

CHAPTER ONE

We're Always At Choice

In 1979, I learned a valuable lesson about how fragile life is. That year, within ten months of a fun visit in March to Florida's Disney World with my wife, Shirley, and our four children, she died from acute myeloblastic leukemia (AML) at thirty-nine years of age. She died the day after Christmas, and I became a widower with children ranging in age from nine to sixteen.

The country was in trouble economically. Within two weeks of my wife's funeral, I was told to terminate ten people in my marketing department. Within five months, my job was eliminated, and I was told to find another position within the company where I'd worked for over eighteen years. That same day, the president of the company froze all personnel requisitions.

Here was my situation: I was forty-one years old, had no wife, no money, four children to raise without a partner, many losses, and no job, and unemployment was at 10–12 percent. I was scared.

One day all the stress and loss combined, and I broke down in tears at the office. I left early to see if my parents could care for my kids. I wanted to escape on a solo trip to sort out my life. My father suggested I contact the company to see if they could help. I had access to the company psychiatrist, so I called him. He made time to see me that afternoon. After I explained my situation, he asked if I'd be willing to place myself in the psych ward of a local hospital that afternoon.

I said, "You bet!"

Fortunately, I had learned how to use professional consultants in my business life, so I didn't see any stigma in asking for help in my personal life. I was relieved I was going to get some help.

My new beginning started in the psych ward in June 1980 with a diagnosis of *situational depression*. Within a few days, when the nursing staff tallied my loss and stress points, I learned I was off the charts, and no one was surprised I was asking for help. Except me. There was a good reason no one was surprised to see me: Stress experts say that if you have 100 loss or stress points, there's a 50 percent chance something physically will go amiss in your body. At 300 loss/stress points, there's an 80 percent chance something will go. When they tallied my loss points for six months, I exceeded 500 loss/stress points.

Life changed for me with Shirley's death. The sun still rose every day, but that phase of my life, being married, living with Shirley, and raising our children together, was over.

A big realization for me in my life journey is that life is short. Life is shorter for some than for others. Unfortunately, there are no do-overs. *This is it!* If life throws you curveballs or you've made a wrong decision, you must accept what's happened and move on. If you've lost a loved one, you must accept what happened and move on.

I'm not saying we can get by without grieving. If we're genuinely loving and compassionate people, we suffer whenever we lose someone or something we care about. My point is that our own lifetime is limited, and life continues while we're grieving.

I don't believe we're responsible for the things that happen to us outside our control, like hurricanes, tsunamis, the death of a mate, the loss of a relationship, or diseases like COVID-19. Still, I believe we are accountable and responsible for what we create in our lives, and we are *always at choice* regarding how we handle situations.

I speak about my life before and after forty. The gift my wife gave me with her life was the opportunity to learn that I am *always at choice*, and I can choose to live joyfully and in gratitude rather than in sadness and depression.

My turning point came from an experience in the psych ward.

The occupational therapy selected for me was learning how to cook again. I had cooked for six months when I was ten, and my mother was in the hospital with Guillain-Barré syndrome (GBS), a disorder in which one's immune system attacks their nerves. In high school, I earned money as a fry cook and later managed and cooked at the Glacier National Park coffee shop. I did well with hamburgers, cheeseburgers, eggs, pancakes, chili, and roast beef, but it had been years since I'd cooked a full meal.

The condition of the occupational therapy lesson was that I had to follow a recipe and *do it right*.

I decided to bake a chicken and ordered all the materials. I took the materials into my cooking room. After what seemed like a couple of hours of chopping celery, onions, liver, and heart, and boiling them to make the broth for the dressing, I found myself getting angrier and angrier—with a French knife in my hand. I was concerned I might hurt myself or someone else.

I asked to see someone, and they sent me to my room to wait for a consulting nurse.

The nurse came into my room and said cheerily, "Hello, Larry, I hear you're having a bit of a struggle. What's happening?"

I responded angrily, "I've just spent two hours preparing this GD chicken for baking, and that's how I'm going to live the rest of my life. Cooking for my kids!"

She said, "Well, Larry, it sounds to me like you're going to have to grow up."

I blew up and started sharing information to establish that I was grown up: "I'm forty-one years old, have four kids, been a leader of Toastmasters, Kiwanis, and American Field Service, and I'm a marketing manager of a major Fortune 500 company."

And she said, "What I'm trying to say is: *You're always at choice.*"

Still angry, I responded, "It's not a choice. I *have to* take care of my kids." My father had cared for me, my brother, and my sister when my mother was hospitalized for six months. He was my model.

Patiently and respectfully, she offered alternatives: I could have my folks watch over my kids. I could send my kids to schools where they could stay in residence. I could split the kids up and have my relatives care for them. I could send my kids to foster homes.

Finally, to get her off my back, I said, "All right, *I choose* to take care of my kids."

And she said, "Good. Now, you can *choose* how you cook for your kids. You can cook for your kids, hire someone to cook for your kids, purchase prepared meals, or hire someone to teach your kids how to cook."

And I got it! I was *at choice* regarding how I cared for my kids and how I cooked for my kids—and I was *always at choice* regarding how I looked at life's problems. I could need to, want to, have to, get to, choose to do something. If I *chose to* do something, I am in control versus being forced by *needing to*, *having to*, or *wanting to*. *Getting to* allows me to feel grateful for the opportunity, but *choosing to* is the most positive, forwarding statement for me.

I wish I could say I only had to learn this lesson once, but I've been reminded throughout my life that I'm *always at choice* regarding my life decisions. I've had many other turning points in my life and have benefited from a lot of good help and assistance, but this lesson that I'm *always at choice* laid a foundation.

Today, because of my choices, I have a lovely relationship with my second wife, Dodie, and we've been together for more than thirty years. My children adore her.

I'm happy to report that all four of my children have graduated from the college of their choice and are all living satisfying and fulfilling lives with everyday life-learning opportunities.

After leaving the company where I worked for over eighteen years, I joined another Fortune 500 company for five years. I then went on to create my own strategic planning facilitation business, Business Development Specialists. My business is now called Stepping Through the Gate, and my focus is helping individuals with significant loss or setbacks in their lives gain clarity regarding their situation, accept it, and move on to capitalize on their new life possibilities.

No matter how bad things seem, we're *always at choice* regarding our actions. Rather than looking at our lives as something we *need to do* or *have to* do, we're much more successful and happier if we *choose to* do the task.

CHAPTER TWO

Guiding Beliefs and Values

The following ideas became the guiding beliefs and values by which I chose to live my life after my first wife died. As I said in my introduction, I am sharing my insights about life to help you more fully live yours.

Twelve Big Life Lessons

These are the core lessons I've learned to date. I hope you can use these ideas to create a rich, enjoyable, satisfying, and fulfilling life journey for yourself. Please take what you can use and leave the rest.

1. We're *always at choice.*
   - I am *always at choice* regarding how I handle a change or situation.
   - Even the choice of not making a choice is a choice.
   - I've found I'm much more effective when I say, "I *choose* to" do something rather than "I *need* to," "I *have* to," "I *want* to," and "I *get* to."

- When I "choose to" do something, I'm in control and the one with power. I take more decisive action from that position.
- How I look at things is critical. If I change my view, I can change what I see.
- Life is short. Remember the discerning questions: *How Much Time Do I Have Left?* and *Am I using it wisely?*

2. We're accountable and responsible for what we create in our lives.
   - I don't believe I'm responsible for things outside my control, like hurricanes, tsunamis, life-termination illnesses, COVID-19, the death of a mate, the death of a child, the death of a pet, or war.
   - I believe I am *always at choice* regarding how I respond to things outside my control.
   - Life comes to me; I can decide how to deal with it—it is my choice.
   - I choose not to live my life as a victim.

3. Our moods and emotions are predispositions for the actions we take.
   - I am accountable and responsible for creating and choosing the moods I live in.
   - I choose to live my life with an *Attitude of Gratitude* and to celebrate my blessings.
   - The mood I'm in affects the actions I can take.
   - I can do more by being optimistic and positive versus depressed and negative.
   - I choose: "beautiful state" over "suffering state" to avoid emotional spirals. Emotional spiraling is a

process in which one negative thought or feeling triggers a cascade of increasingly intense and distressing emotions. It's like a snowball rolling down a hill, gathering more snow and momentum as it descends.

- Living in gratitude is a good mood choice.
- The popular metaphor of the Two Wolves is a good reminder of which wolf I chose to feed. The metaphor is that each of us has within us two fighting wolves—one who is guided by fear and anger (negative thoughts), another who is guided by love and kindness (positive thoughts). The wolf I choose to feed is the one who survives the fight.
- I can decide to be grateful, joyful, and blessed, or frustrated, angry, and scared.

4. I choose to live a life of gratitude and to appreciate blessings.
    - It's much easier to do new things when I'm grateful for what I already have.
    - Learning to live in gratitude and honor my accomplishments is an integral part of my life journey.
    - I like thinking in terms of *Blessings*: My version of Blessings is that they are *gifts* that come to me that I don't have any control over, like sunshine, rain, flowers, leaves turning colors, trees, animals, horses, squirrels, birds, bird songs, colors, sounds, and many other of nature's wonders. These are an example of things I am easily grateful for. They are indeed gifts over which I have no control.
    - I exchange ten Blessings a day with a selected group of friends. That means I may see an additional thirty

or forty blessings daily. Seeing their Blessings has a positive impact on my mood.
- My driving force is to live my life in joy, peace, and serenity.

5. We can creatively capitalize on our Natural Gifts and Talents wherever they take us (where our values align).
   - I'm at my best when I focus on creatively capitalizing on my natural gifts and talents wherever they take me, not my developed skill sets.
   - My lifetime purpose is to be in service to others with my natural gifts and talents where our values align.
   - Prioritize: Focus on the 20 percent that makes 80 percent of the difference, also known as the *Pareto Principle*. In other words, work on the big rocks first. If you don't work on the big problems first, you won't be able to find the time to work on them later because you've used up your time on less important things.
   - Be accountable (*accountability* is explored in more detail in the next chapter), which includes four important steps, namely: 1) Seeing the problem, 2) Taking responsibility for solving the problem, 3) Investing the time and energy to solve the problem, 4) Taking the action necessary to solve the problem.
   - I love my mate, my family, my friends, and my opportunities to be of service.

6. Trust is critical for success in relationships and business teams, and it is imperative for high-performing organizations.

7. I believe we create our reality in language.
   - Understanding how to make and manage promises is essential to creating and maintaining trust.
   - In my experience, it's been vital to learn Linguistic Distinctions (See Chapter Six: Language for Action and Results). These are the six primary Linguistic Acts according to Drs. Fernando Flores and Mathew Budd:
     o Declarations
     o Assessments
     o Assertions
     o Requests
     o Offers
     o Promises

8. Being "of service" is my fundamental life choice. Being of service doesn't work for everyone as a life purpose, but it works for me.
   - It's critical for people to feel connected, valued, and appreciated.
   - A successful way to fulfill this need is to choose a fulfilling purpose and to serve others.
   - Living my life on purpose is my choice.
   - Research suggests that by being of service to others, I can extend my life seven to eight years.

9. Commitment to lifelong learning is essential.
   - A commitment to lifelong learning is essential to remain flexible and adaptable, and to deal effectively with the many expected and unexpected changes guaranteed to appear in my life.

- The more I know, the more I know I don't know.
- It's beneficial to be curious.
- There are always opportunities for learning new methods, skills, and mindsets.

10. It's crucial to learn how to accept loss and deal with grief.
    - Learn the stages of grieving:
      o Disbelief/Denial
      o Yearning
      o Bargaining
      o Anger/Resentment
      o Sadness/Depression/Resignation
      o Acceptance (Moving On)/Plan for the Future
    - The graphic "The Whirlpool of Grief," found in Chapter Ten, is an excellent depiction of what it's like to experience grief.
    - Once the loss is accepted, choose to move on and devise a plan for the future.
    - It's important to remember:
      o Life is not a dress rehearsal. This is it!
      o Life is short.
      o There are no do-overs, no mulligans.

11. Learning how to ask for help and support is vital.
    - I learned how to ask for help in both my personal and professional life.
    - I learned I didn't have to have all the answers.
    - I learned I can move better and faster with help than without to solve a challenging problem or issue or capitalize on an opportunity.

- It was necessary for me to let go of my ego to ask for help!
- I can use the wisdom of the group to solve difficult issues.

12. The business should work for me; I should not work for the business. I work with individuals, business owners, and entrepreneurs who choose to live fully engaged lives while creating their income.

A Word About Play

An additional value I've come to appreciate later in life is the importance of Play. I learned this lesson in the Milford Sound of New Zealand. In my opinion, Milford Sound is one of the most beautiful places I've experienced in the world, especially after a rainstorm, when all the waterfalls are flowing. During my first boat ride, I noticed that all the Americans traveling were either eighteen or nineteen years old, with a body, but no money, traveling on a shoestring; or they were seventy or eighty years old, with money, but no body to hike mountains and enjoy the New Zealand experience. They could only view it.

All the Asians or Europeans on the boat were in their forties. I realized that in America, our vacation concepts were screwed up. After the Milford Sound experience, I declared I would take three vacations a year. As an independent entrepreneur I could do it and did. I will always be grateful for that choice. I've learned that if I don't have play in my life, I will eventually get grumpy and resentful of the fact that life is all work and no play.

This I Believe: Living On Purpose

Over time, I've collected the essential beliefs that guide my life. This list is also available on my website, larryfreeborg.com.

I believe there is a higher power, something greater than me, which is responsible for this beautiful world I live in. Birds, flowers, colors, mountains, trees, the air I breathe, music, art, water in its many forms, and animals are but a few things that come to me that I don't have control over.

I believe in living in gratitude for the things that come to me that I don't have any control of (I call them *Blessings*). Living in gratitude opens me up to recognize, acknowledge, and contribute the gifts that I am.

I believe that everyone has been given a gift/talent, something that's unique to them. Our role in life is to discover our gifts and determine how we can best contribute to the well-being of mankind through capitalizing on our gifts.

I believe experience is the best teacher, but this doesn't mean the experience always has to be mine. My role is to be curious, open, and willing to listen to and learn from teachers who have experienced many things before me.

I believe beliefs guide our lives. Beliefs that have been informed by parents, churches, schools, friends, media, government, teachers, mentors, our experiences and the choices we make about the experience. Some belief systems help us move forward and some belief systems hold us back.

I believe that the two most powerful acts are forgiveness and letting go. Through the rapid release of judgment, anger, and resentment, I am able to move forward positively in being the gift I am with peace, joy, and serenity.

My life exploration has been to discover the ways that belief systems can be changed, shifted, and altered to enable people to be the gift they are to live happy and fully engaged lives.

To review, these twelve beliefs guide how I've chosen to live my life. They've provided a strong foundation that has enabled me to create a rich, enjoyable, satisfying, and fulfilling life journey.

My concise list of critical beliefs and values:

1. I'm *always at choice.*
2. I'm accountable and responsible for what I create in my life.
3. My moods and emotions are predispositions for the actions I take.
4. I live my life in gratitude and appreciate my blessings. My driving force (super goal) is to live my life in joy, peace, and serenity.
5. I creatively capitalize on my Natural Gifts and Talents wherever they take me (where my values align).
6. Trust is critical for my success in relationships and business teams and is imperative for high-performing organizations.
7. I believe we create rather than describe our reality in Language. It's important to understand how to make and manage promises to create and maintain trust.
8. Being of service is my fundamental "way of life" choice.
9. My commitment to lifelong learning has been essential.
10. It's been crucial for me to learn how to accept and process loss and deal with grief.
11. Learning how to ask for help and support has been very important for my success.
12. I learned my business should work for me; I should not work for my business.

CHAPTER THREE

Accountability and Responsibility

Life comes to me—I can decide how to deal with it. It's my choice.

It took me a while to learn this lesson. Five years after my wife's death, I was still struggling to put my life back together. I first heard about accountability and responsibility in a program called Lifespring, a human potential organization that offered large group training similar to est (Erhard Seminars Training, marketed as *est*, though often encountered as *Est* or *EST*).

I had heard about est, but I thought Lifespring would be a better choice because they didn't limit your trips to the bathroom. However, Lifespring began their workshops with the same approach as est. First, they reviewed the guidelines for the meeting.

Est's guidelines required participants to agree to follow the ground rules, which included not wearing watches, not talking until called upon, not talking to their neighbors, and not eating or leaving their seats to go to the bathroom except during breaks separated by many hours.

Lifespring was founded in 1974 by John Hanley Sr., Robert White, Randy Revell, and Charlene Afremow as a for-profit human potential organization. Lifespring would later be surrounded by controversy in the 1970s and 1980s, with accusations of the training methods as deceptive and controlling. Allegations arose that Lifespring was a cult that used coercive methods to prevent members from leaving. While this may have been true for some people, I found the personal work I did in Lifespring very helpful in my recovery journey.

None of this controversy was apparent when I heard about Lifespring, so I signed up immediately for the training in Denver, Colorado, rather than waiting for the program to come to Minneapolis. However, I had difficulty adjusting to the guidelines at the initial group meeting in Denver because they introduced something I hadn't heard before when I originally signed up for the training.

The condition for taking the course was that I had to show up in Denver ten days after the initial training for a follow-up session. I was irritated because I hadn't been told about that condition before I signed up for the workshop and spent the money to fly there. It was being presented as a condition I'd have to fulfill if I wanted to take the course. The condition was that I couldn't continue the course if I didn't commit to making it back for the follow-up.

When this guideline was initially introduced, I thought there was no way I would be able to fulfill that commitment. After a very intense, interactive dialogue with the trainer in front of 120 people, the trainer asked me, "Would you agree to consider the possibility of being in Denver ten days from now, and if so—if you could be here—would you attend?" After reflecting on the option, I agreed, and the minute I agreed there was a possibility I would attend, my mood shifted.

My conflict with returning for the follow-up session was that I had a trade show scheduled at West Point, New York, military academy that started the day after I was scheduled to be in Denver. I didn't know how to get to Denver, make the Lifespring meeting, and then fly to the U.S. Military Academy at West Point in time.

It turned out that once I was willing to consider that I might be able to make it, I looked at the travel schedules and found a red-eye flight that would get into West Point in time for me to work the trade show.

I would have someone set up the exhibit so it would be ready for me when I arrived.

We are accountable and responsible for what we create.
Be an Observer of the Observer You Are.

This experience taught me to question my thoughts about what's possible. If I could open to the possibility, all sorts of circumstances and events could fall into place and become real.

That part of the lesson with Lifespring was very useful. However, their idea of keeping commitments didn't work well for me. From their perspective, you either kept the commitment or you didn't. There was no flexibility to manage a commitment.

Lifespring used many English words in a manner different from their usual meaning. *Commitment*, for instance, was defined as "the willingness to do whatever it takes."

I learned there was an alternative way to look at a situation when I attended Newfield Network, an organization dedicated to personal development, coach training and certification, and leadership training. I realized there are situations when it's impossible to keep a commitment. For example, let's say I have two meetings scheduled at the same time for some reason. I'd have to cancel or renegotiate one of the meetings. I call this *managing my commitments*, and now that I've learned how to have *conversations for action or results*, I call it *managing my promises*. Managing my promises became a new focus in my life, including arriving at meetings on time and respecting others who arrived on time.

When I introduced promise management to my clients, it made a tremendous difference in their mood of trust within the business and overall performance. Broken promises bring a lack of trust, resulting in poor performance and negative impact on an employees' sense of well-being.

Accountability has become a buzzword in business, but unfortunately, most of the time it has come to mean penalizing someone for making a mistake or not keeping a commitment. It didn't stand for not managing a promise. My perspective changed when I was exposed to the book *The Oz Principle*. Written by Roger Connors, Tom Smith, and Craig Hickman, it was first published in 1994. Rising above your circumstances to get the results you seek is the empowering principle operating in Frank Baum's Land of Oz, explored in his series of children's books. *The Oz Principle* discusses leadership, accountability, and results and has the most useful definition of Accountability for me.

The Oz Principle's Definition of Accountability

Our interpretation of *accountability* can move beyond a punitive, blaming context to one of taking responsibility for one's actions and abilities. That is the definition of Accountability excerpted from *The Oz Principle: Getting Results Through Individual and Organizational Accountability*, by Connors, Smith, and Hickman, paraphrased here.

Being accountable means:

- Adopting an attitude of continually asking: *What else can I do to rise above my circumstances and achieve the results I desire?*
- Engaging in the Steps to Accountability, 1) Seeing it, 2) Owning it, 3) Solving it and 4) Doing it.
- Accepting ownership that includes making, keeping, and proactively answering for personal commitments.
- Embracing both current and future efforts rather than reactive and historical explanations.

Above and Below the Line

The Oz Principle defines *Above the Line®* thinking as following the Steps to Accountability: When we are functioning Above the Line, we are doing all the things listed above.

The Oz Principle also defines when someone is not being Accountable and living as a victim as *Below the Line®* thinking. This is when we aren't taking accountability, and we focus on things we can't control. We play the blame game, are reactive, and externalize the need for change.

They describe the characteristics of Below the Line thinking as follows:

1. Ignore/Deny
2. It's Not My Job
3. Finger Pointing
4. Confusion and Tell Me What to Do
5. Cover Your Tail
6. Wait and See

When I learned about these practices, what amazed me was that I could tell by how people acted and spoke whether they were operating accountably (Above the Line) or as victims (Below the Line).

To learn this approach to Accountability, I recommend reading or listening to *The Oz Principle*, reviewing the online videos, and doing the workshop.

History of Large Group Awareness Programs

Large group awareness programs came under a lot of public scrutiny during my lifetime, and in several cases, were labeled by some as *nonreligious cults*. The controversy has resulted in several of these organizations going out of business or being reconfigured. With my writing about these courses, I'm not suggesting other people consider taking these courses. I am reporting how these learnings were helpful for me, the decisions I made about the belief systems they were imparting, which beliefs I accepted, and which beliefs I determined didn't work for me. Where the belief didn't work for me, I committed to finding an alternative way of looking at the situation.

Lifespring went defunct in the 1990s. The director of corporate affairs, Charles "Raz" Ingrasci, joined the Hoffman Institute, which uses many of the same principles today.

Erhard Seminars Training, or est, was an organization founded by Werner Erhard in 1971. It offered a two-weekend (six-day, sixty-hour) course known officially as The Est Standard Training. The seminar aimed to transform one's ability to experience living so the situations one had been trying to change or had been putting up with cleared up in the process of life itself. An est website claims that the training brought ideas of transformation, personal responsibility, accountability, and possibility to the forefront. Est became The Forum, Landmark Education, and Landmark Worldwide.

My key learnings about accountability include:

1. Managing my promises well creates trust in personal and business relationships.
2. Making a clear request with a timetable for completion secures a promise I can manage effectively.
3. Before making a request, I need to know whether the person I've made a request of has the authority and power to make a decision to solve the problem.
4. Accountability doesn't have to mean someone gets fired. It's more important that people make, keep, and proactively answer for their personal commitments.
5. How I regard the problem could be part of the problem.
6. "I'm *always at choice*" and "I'm accountable and responsible for what I create in my life" have been my core foundational beliefs.

CHAPTER FOUR

Be an Observer of the Observer You Are

Julio Ollala, CEO emeritus and primary teacher of The Newfield Network, started many of his presentations with the phrase: *Be an observer of the observer you are.* The first time I was introduced to this concept, I needed help understanding it. What was my teacher trying to tell me?

Look at the way you're looking at the action you're taking to achieve the result you're trying to achieve.

I didn't understand that how I looked at a problem could be the problem. Julio helped me understand how I viewed the world could be the problem. Again, this is a reminder of the exposure I had gained to this approach while in the psych ward, as well as in the work for personal and professional growth in Lifespring, Richard Strozzi Heckler (Strozzi Institute), Onsite, Byron Katie (The Work), and now Shirzad Chamine (Positive Intelligence).

By becoming an observer of the observer I was, I realized that many of the belief systems I had been using had come from my parents, my religion, my relatives, the school that I went to, my teachers, my friends, my neighbors, the media, books I'd read, the movies I'd seen, the government, and beliefs I'd made up from the experiences I had and on how I viewed the situation. I began to realize that all my beliefs were my choices.

I could ask myself of each belief system: *Is this helping me solve the problem, or is it hindering me from solving the problem?*

Before I was exposed to this concept, I believed that if I wanted a different result, I had to put more effort into my actions or take another, more decisive action. Many of us were told in our youth that if we wanted a different result, we just needed to work harder. This is what I now call *First-Order Learning*: staying focused on Actions and Results.

Learning About Learning – First-Order Learning

Traditional learning dictates that if we change the action, we create different results.

The graphic below shows how I used to approach solving problems. If I wasn't getting the desired results, I'd put more effort into the actions I took to achieve them.

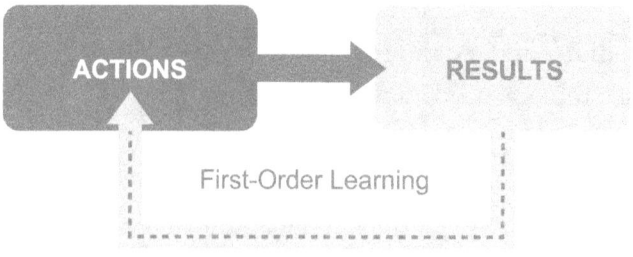

Julio's teaching opened me up to understand how I looked at solving the problem was based on my beliefs. My new objective was to determine whether my views were helping me solve the problem or hindering me from solving the problem. It became essential for me to look at where my beliefs came from.

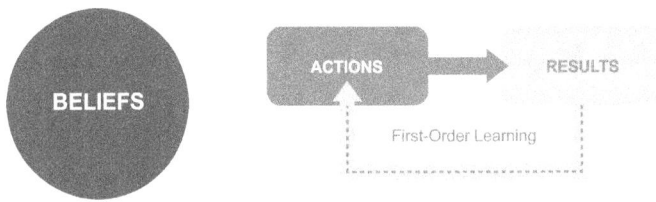

Beliefs result from our learning as a child and as adults. Our assumptions and beliefs impact our ability to act. Shifting our beliefs can open opportunities to act and to create different results. There are many sources for our beliefs. Depending on our history and experiences, some are much more potent than others.

Here is a list of sources for our beliefs and influences on our thoughts:

Sources & Influences

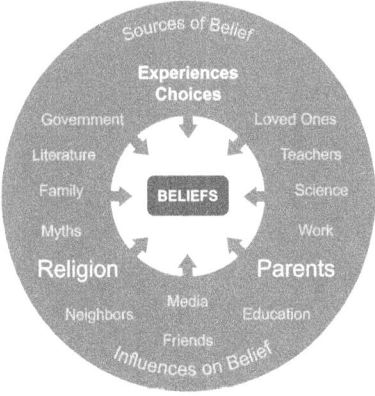

Observe Your Beliefs—
Are they helping or hindering?

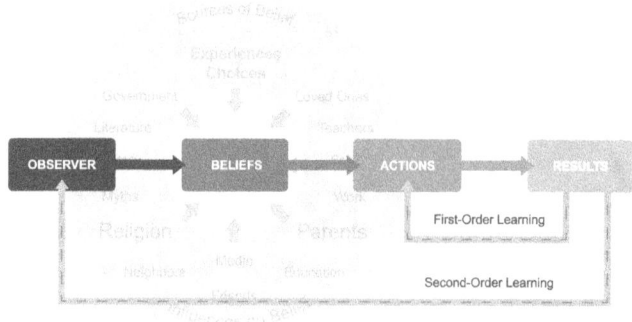

As we become more proficient in observing of our beliefs, we would label this as *Second-Order Learning*. When we become proficient in being an Observer of our Beliefs we can observe the entire sequence, as a Meta-Observer.

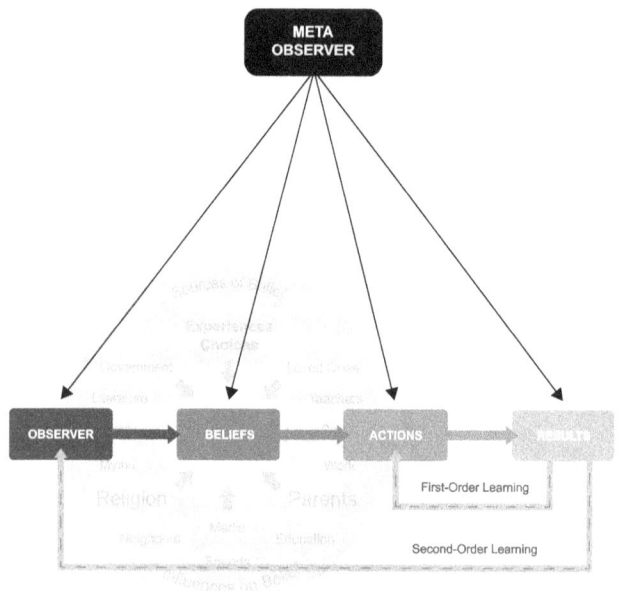

Checking Questions

In addition to keeping this model in mind, I ask myself these questions to establish whether I'm on the right track:

1. *Are the results what I'm really looking for?*
2. *Will my actions create results as I want them to, or could I take other actions? What if I think outside the box?*
3. *Are my beliefs the best ideas possible, or should I consider other belief systems to improve my results?*

Taking the approach of being an observer of the observer I am, I've realized people I often work with could take a different action only after they changed their belief systems. They were blocked, stuck, and unable to see the possible options based on their limiting belief systems. This is where Second-Order Learning comes in.

When I considered people's beliefs about their actions, the connection between their views and their achievements became even more evident. It was highly revealing that people had different perspectives about what was possible based on their personal histories and experiences.

Changing My Beliefs

Besides learning how to take care of my kids after my wife passed away, developing a mature love relationship became my biggest challenge. In my learning journey, I discovered the problem I was having in relationships after my wife's passing was the choice I had unconsciously made about my mother's illness, Guillain-Barré syndrome, which is a rare condition that causes a person's immune system to attack their peripheral nerves, resulting in partial loss of sensation, loss of movement, and even changes in cognitive ability and personality. My brother, sister, and I would poke needles in my mom's arms and legs to see if she could feel them and to see if she was getting better.

My high school sweetheart, who I thought I would marry, left me to go to Washington, D.C. As a result of her leaving, I joined up with the Air Force Reserves for seven and one-half years, thinking she was coming back after six months. I never saw her again.

Later, Shirley's death reinforced the limiting belief I had adopted when my mother was sick. That belief was: *I can trust the woman I love to leave me.* I had first made up the belief then, but I was living with the thought at age fifty-five as if it were still the truth.

Putting together another loving, caring relationship after Shirley's death was tied up in many unhealthy belief systems from my past. I did a lot of work in Adult Children of Alcoholics, Lifespring, and other workshops and worked with several counselors to solve this problem, but I eventually got the most help from one of the world's leading therapeutic centers, Onsite Workshops.

Founded by Sharon Wegscheider-Cruse and Joe Cruse, Onsite is now based in Cumberland Furnace, Tennessee. Sharon was also the cofounder of Adult Children of Alcoholics, and Joe Cruse set up the Betty Ford Treatment Center.

At Onsite, I got in touch with my limiting beliefs about the women I loved. The belief I had was crazy-making for the women I dated because I would have the *come here, come here; go away, I don't trust you* syndrome left over from my experience with my mom being sick. After a psychodrama experience at Onsite, I now believe the women I love do not leave me. I think of them almost every day. Indeed, although the women's love I reflect on is not physically available anymore, I regularly relive fond memories of my time with them.

I'm very happy to report that, since my Onsite Living Center Program and a couple of additional Onsite programs, I've been in a loving, supportive relationship with my life partner, Dodie, for over thirty years. With her help and guidance, we've raised six healthy and prosperous adults: my four children and her two. My children adore her.

One of the best processes I've found to help people change their view of their circumstances is The Work, described by Byron Katie in her book, *Loving What Is* (Harmony Books, 2002). In her process, she takes people through a thinking journey that helps them shift their belief systems. She also provides excellent support for her approach on her website, thework.com, with videos demonstrating how the thinking journey works.

My learning journey to develop alternative belief systems that work better for me has included the book *Psycho-Cybernetics* (Simon and Schuster, 1960) by Maxwell Maltz; attending Adult Children of Alcoholics meetings for five years; completing six programs of Lifespring; six programs at Onsite including their Living Centered Program and psychodrama training; multiple sessions, including two trips to Chile, of the Newfield Network Ontological Coaching; somatic programs and various programs of the Strozzi Institute; Equine Guided Coaching with numerous teachers, including a trip to Germany; a Byron Katie workshop and videos; three programs with Tony Robbins; and Positive Intelligence training with Shirzad Chamine.

In summary, the learning journey I've been on has helped me develop the belief systems I'm sharing with you. These new beliefs worked for me to have the quality of life I have today.

The most significant barrier I've found in coaching people through only words is having them realize and accept their belief systems. People spin their stories very fast. The belief they are living with is something they've chosen, and they can choose something else when they think it would better serve them.

Be sure to check on your beliefs and see where they have come from. Determine whether they are the beliefs you want to live by today.

Best wishes for success in finding beliefs that will work for you when you review how you observe your circumstances. I hope you will also discover which beliefs hinder your progress and replace them.

CHAPTER FIVE

Creatively Capitalize on Natural Gifts and Talents

I'm a committed lifelong learner. Not the traditional university learning, but the commitment to always be curious. Ongoing learning became another key foundation of my life.

My first major lesson after college involved creatively capitalizing on my natural gifts and talents, not the skillsets or things I'd learned and been taught how to do. I was twenty-seven years old, working as a sales rep for the 3M Company in Milwaukee, Wisconsin. I was selling graphic art supplies through dealers. I was doing okay in my career but felt called to give more presentations in my work, so I decided to join Toastmasters, a nonprofit educational group that teaches public speaking and leadership in a supportive environment.

Fortunately for me, the club I chose to join was an older, well-established club with seasoned members. Not only did I learn about public speaking, but a lot of other good ideas were shared. We took on tough subjects in what are called *Table Topics*, so I became more confident and comfortable expressing my thoughts. I also took on responsibilities within the club, so I grew as a leader.

One evening, a fellow Toastmaster shared that one of the influential books he was reading was Maltz's *Psycho-Cybernetics* (Simon & Schuster, 1960). I purchased the book, and Dr. Maltz's ideas and insights started me on my lifelong learning journey.

About the same time, another fellow Toastmaster announced he had just been promoted to plant manager of a primary manufacturing plant in the area. I congratulated him on his success and found the courage to ask him, "To what do you attribute your success?"

His response is with me to this day.

He said, "You know, Larry, I'm not a very smart guy. In fact, I didn't finish high school. Eventually, I got my GED in the service, and I tried a couple of courses in college, but they didn't seem to fit very well either." He went on to say, "But, in the area of production planning, I'm not trying to be braggadocious; it just happens to be the way it is. I think three-to-four times faster than the people that are next to me.

"So, this is what I think is the secret to success. First: Find your natural gift and talents. Your true gifts and talents are not your skillset or what you've learned or been taught how to do. Second: Be creative in your gifted area. And, many people have many great ideas, but they don't do anything with them. The most important step is third: Implement your creations."

I said thanks for the info and left that meeting in deep thought. I felt I was a jack-of-all-trades but a master of none. I thought I was reasonably bright, but I didn't know what my natural gifts and talents were.

I contemplated the question: *What are my natural gifts and talents?*

That evening, I declared from then on, I would creatively capitalize on my natural gifts and talents, wherever they would take me. I'm happy to report it's been an incredible life journey.

I must admit. It took me a while to discover my gifts— about six months. I initially found my gifts by exploring the places where I had achieved considerable success and had the most fun in my job, areas where I lost track of time and would work beyond the call of duty to do a job well.

Shortly after, I found several life-planning books supporting this concept of finding and capitalizing on gifts and talents. One of the best life-planning books I used was *Where Do I Go from Here with My Life? A Systematic, Practical, and Effective Life/Work Planning Manual for Students, Instructors, Counselors, Career Seekers, and Career Changers*, by John C. Crystal and Richard N. Bolles (Ten Speed Press, 1974). Unfortunately, it's out of print now.

Another life-planning book that, after fifty years, is quite popular and highly recommended is *What Color is Your Parachute?* by Richard N. Bolles (Ten Speed Press, 1970). In promotional material, it's been cited as "having transformed the way people think about job hunting."

Today almost all life-planning processes start with an assignment to discover your natural gifts and talents. Now many of them also include an exercise to identify your Core Values.

I augmented all my life-planning work with several assessment tools. The most effective assessment tool for me was the *Highlands Ability Battery*. The Battery tested things that I couldn't prepare for ahead of time. It is designed to identify gifts. In that assessment, I learned I see patterns at the 97th percentile and can describe them so others can see them at a very practical level. This knowledge reinforced my belief in my facilitation skills which I was using in my strategic business planning sessions with groups.

More Assessment Tools

The DISC Model. This simple yet powerful tool for assessing human behavior is based on personality traits and describes four basic styles:

- Dominance
- Influence
- Conscientiousness
- Steadiness

Different people approach life differently. We all develop our style, and for the most part, we stick with it. Understanding our style can be enormously helpful while learning to interact more effectively with others who may not share our style.

Another assessment tool that intrigues me has recently been introduced. It is called *Working Geniuses* by Patrick Lencioni. This assessment tool starts with the premise that everyone has a genius place. We are doing genius things when we do something that comes naturally to us. There are also things we've learned to do well but don't necessarily enjoy, and things we may have learned to do but do not like to do. I've found this assessment tool to be very affirming and helpful; however, I didn't get exposed to this assessment until later in my life.

In addition, I've been blessed in both my personal life and my income journey by the tragedies and opportunities I've chosen to learn from. The choice to learn has improved the lives of my family, my clients, and myself.

I spent over twenty-three years working for two outstanding Fortune 500 companies, 3M Company and Medtronic, primarily in business development (sales and marketing).

For the last thirty-plus years, I've created income by facilitating people through strategic business planning sessions and life transformation coaching.

I learned a lot from my significant personal tragedy at age forty. If you recall, my wife contracted leukemia when she was thirty-nine years old and died the day after Christmas in 1979. Sadly, she left me with four young children to raise, and I had no money and no job in the middle of a recession. The event triggered my quest for learning.

I've learned from the experiences of being let go from corporate jobs and consulting engagements. I've used the losses as opportunities to learn new things and to choose what's next.

Today I'm blessed to have a lovely relationship with my second wife, Dodie. We've been together more than thirty years. This accomplishment has required my learning how to change my beliefs.

Re*fire*ment

Recently I rejoined Toastmasters. You may be wondering why, at eighty-six, I would. I did so to refresh my public speaking skills and fulfill my current Refirement life objectives. *Refirement* is a word I created to describe how I intend to approach retirement. I had looked at the word *retire* in the dictionary, and the descriptions were not very inspiring for me. I've enjoyed what I've done for work and found no reason to stop. My idea was to get re-energized about it again, refired, so to speak. I definitely have not chosen to retire.

My refirement goals:
1. Finish writing and publishing my book
2. Give presentations regarding the life lessons I've learned along my life journey

Let me leave you with these thoughts:

If you commit to creatively capitalize on your natural gifts and talents, wherever they take you—where your values align—there is an excellent chance you will enjoy a life of satisfaction, achievement, and fulfillment in being of service to others.

Research suggests that if you're serving others, there is an excellent chance you will extend your life from seven-and-one-half to eight years. Your job is to find your gifts.

Do not be afraid to use the talents you possess.

It's well worth your time to search out and find your gift, talents, and values.

The woods would be very silent if no birds sang except those who sang the best. Comparisons can both inspire or sabotage our journey.

CHAPTER SIX

Section One

Language for Action and Results

It is possible to re-learn how to communicate to bring about better circumstances. How you view language greatly impacts the results you desire to achieve. These are critical pieces of learning I've carried forward since reading *You Are What You Say* by Matthew Budd and Larry Rothstein (Penguin Random House, 2001). In it, there is a section of a chapter that I've read repeatedly. It offers a new way of looking at language based on ideas the author learned from Dr. Fernando Flores.

Unfortunately, I never had the opportunity to meet Dr. Flores personally. I haven't gone to any of his workshops. I hadn't read any of the material he wrote until his daughter published a summary of his thoughts in a book called *Conversations for Action and Collected Essays*, edited by Maria Flores Letelier (CreateSpace Independent Publishing Platform, 2013).

As it turns out, there are five additional avenues through which Dr. Flores's work has significantly influenced my beliefs about language and life:

45

1. Multiple LifeSpring workshops I attended and staffed in 1984 and 1985.
2. A software called The Coordinator, developed by Action Technology (Fernando Flores's company), which I helped install for a client of mine.
3. Multiple trainings presented by Julio Olalla and Rafael Echeverria of Newfield Network, including a couple workshops in Chile. I attended Ontological Coaching Training at Newfield Network for two years and helped staff several training sessions afterward.
4. Somatic Coaching Training I attended for over two years, put on by Richard Strozzi-Heckler and Staci Haines of the Strozzi Institute.
5. The book *Understanding Computers and Cognition* (Addison-Wesley Professional, 1987), which Flores coauthored with Terry Winograd.

I list my exposure to Dr. Flores's work to share how many opportunities I used to learn about Linguistic Acts. When I was learning the material, I didn't realize how foundational it would become to my thinking and beliefs today.

As I learned about Dr. Flores's life story, it resonated with me because we both had overcome challenging life experiences. In 1973, Flores was Chile's minister of finance and was imprisoned by the dictator Pinochet. He was subjected to mock trials, punished with solitary confinement, and kept from his wife and family of five children for three-and-one-half years. The challenges I faced in 1979 seemed similar but were less severe.

Flores's position attracted Amnesty International. They helped negotiate his release in 1976. He came to the United States, completed a doctorate program at the University of

California at Berkeley, and became a world-famous consultant who used his insights into language to transform companies and people. Flores's work laid the foundation for a lot of the current understandings of action workflow and commitment management theory taught at many leading universities today.

Prison had changed Flores's life. He emerged with a new understanding of the connection between language and actions. What's particularly impressive for me is his statement about imprisonment, which appears attributed to him on countless websites at this point: "I never told a victim story about my imprisonment. Instead, I told a transformation story about how prison changed my outlook and how I saw that communication, truth, and trust are at the heart of power."

While my life is not the same, I've felt that my experience in the psych ward had a similar effect on me. It changed my life. I became keenly aware that I was *always at choice* and needed to find new belief systems to better serve my family and me.

The psych ward experience, combined with the results of a LifeSpring exercise, taught me to view my life not as a victim because of my wife's death but to realize I was at choice regarding how I dealt with it.

Dr. Mathew Budd's story also impressed me. He was trained as a physician and had become frustrated that many of the human problems he dealt with were not diseases like cancer or didn't require surgery. Instead, the patient's thoughts and mindset were creating ill health.

Flores Changed How I Think About Language

In Fernando Flores's concept of *Linguistic Acts*, he identified a new way of communicating and understanding language that I hadn't heard of or experienced before.

When I was going to grade school, the focus on language was learning parts of speech, punctuation, grammar, and so on. Flores labeled specific actions in language which, when used appropriately, helped people communicate more effectively to act and create results. I had previously thought that language was used to describe reality; however, through Flores's teachings, I learned I was creating my reality with language.

Your Speech Greatly Impacts Your Results

The cardinal sin of communication, which compromises all speech and relationships, is assuming that what is said is what is heard.

For example, if I say, "I'm getting a dog," immediately you think of a dog breed you know. Your idea of which dog breed might be far from what I'm considering.

Another example: In meetings I've facilitated, I've asked the participants to think of a *torch*. When I asked people what their image of a torch was, often, everyone had a different idea. The ideas varied from the TV show *Survivor* torch to the Olympic torch. If they were from England, it was a flashlight.

One more example: In my facilitated meetings, I've asked participants to envision a white picket fence. When I asked them to describe an image of their white picket fence, we discovered many different versions, from the fence being one foot to three feet to five feet high. Some fences had tapered tops. Some were rounded or flat, and there was a difference in the spacing of the boards in the fence.

Ask, Observe, Inquire, Discuss, and Listen

Once I realized how often a comment could be misunderstood, I took steps to ensure everyone was talking about the same thing in conversations. I call it a *Background of Obviousness*. In my presentations, I would point out that in every institution there is a background understanding that seems obvious but, in fact, might not be understood by people outside the institution. The words you're using must be understood by the people you're trying to communicate with.

This awareness helped me understand the source of several miscommunications in my business. For example, at one point I was talking about *marketing* with a client, only to realize that when I was using the word *marketing*, the client was thinking of their customer service offer—which they called *marketing*—two completely different topics.

Another term with multiple meanings arose when conversing with a prospective vendor for a company I worked with. They suggested we "needed to do some *benchmarking*." Based on my experience with benchmarking, I anticipated a long process of collecting performance numbers, and the effort would be time consuming and extensive. After a clarifying discussion with the prospective vendor, I found out he was suggesting we visit companies that were models for implementing a certain manufacturing process. This was completely different from what I had been envisioning. By learning what we both meant by *benchmarking*, we were able to agree on what action to take.

Section Two

Conversations for Action and Results

In *You Are What You Say*, Matthew Budd addresses the Conversations for Action and Results. I've found his written definitions of Linguistic Acts to be the best I've come by. I thank him and Penguin Random House for permission to share his work.

Dr. Budd refers to five building blocks. In his list, he sees requests and offers as the same. I see them as different acts, so my list below includes *six* primary Linguistic Acts:

1. Declarations
2. Assessments
3. Assertions
4. Requests
5. Offers
6. Promises

The concepts are simple, but learning the distinctions requires becoming a rigorous observer. It will likely take some time to learn these distinctions; don't expect to learn them instantly. It took practice, and more practice, for me to finally get it.

As I learned what was being said from the linguistic point of view, I saw the impact of using these distinctions. People managed promises, took action, and created results with more respect and a sense of harmony. Eventually, I was able to embody these distinctions. I now employ these without my consciously thinking about them. I encourage you to be patient with yourself in learning these distinctions, and you'll get to the same place I have.

These three core distinctions greatly impacted my life: *Declarations*, *Assessments*, and *Assertions*.

Declarations. A Declaration is an utterance in which someone with the authority to do so brings something into being that wasn't there before.

Declarations that make a difference are made by people with the authority and power to make the Declaration. The Declaration of Independence is an example of this linguistic act. The United States was brought into existence when a group of people empowered to do so declared independence from England. Of course, they had to back up their speaking with many other actions—fighting a war, setting up laws for the new country, and so on. But with the Declaration, they created the possibility for a country.

Declarations are powerful words for me. I see them as being different from goals. They make things happen. Personal Declarations such as "I will complete writing this book by March 15," or "I will listen with more patience to my wife's concerns" can shape our lives if followed with commitment and consistent behavior.

A critical question to consider about declarations is: *Does the person making the Declaration have the authority to make it meaningful?* Another question: *What is this person's commitment to living their life in a way that will fulfill the declaration?*

I completed this book you are reading only due to my Declaration to write and publish my life learning experiences and to share them with others.

Gaining clarity between the following two linguistic acts, Assessments and Assertions, was the most challenging learning for me. It was worth it. The clarity of these distinctions has brought me peace and has become especially useful in my listening to the newscasts of today and group conversations.

Assessments. An Assessment is a judgment that you make about the world in the interest of taking some action. For example, in the interest of going to a football game, I might make the Assessment, "It's a beautiful day," in which there is no wind and the temperature of 65°F is my standard. On the other hand, if I were interested in sailing, my Assessment of "It's a beautiful day" might mean the wind is blowing—and the harder, the better. Beauty as a quality is not in the day itself, but in the eyes of the speaker, determined by their interests and standards.

It was extremely important for me to learn that Assessments are never the Truth. They are interpretations and opinions. They are interpretations people make to fulfill some concerns by their standards.

Assessments are never facts. Remember, they are interpretations and opinions, even though many people may share the same Assessment. Assessments always reveal what's going on for the person or persons making the Assessment.

Assessments may be grounded or not. They can be called *grounded* if there is some evidence on which the Assessment is based, but it's still an Assessment—an interpretation or an opinion.

A person's ability, diligence, and skill in grounding Assessments are essential to be effective in some professions. A doctor, for example, is a person who has learned to make grounded Assessments for the sake of improving patients' health. A lawyer makes grounded Assessments of clients' interests under the law. It all happens in language.

For many of us, our historical narratives are Assessments of ourselves and others: *Others are smarter than I; Others are prettier than I; You can't trust that person; The future is hopeless; So-and-so is a jerk and a con artist.* These Assessments—interpretations and opinions—are often ungrounded, but unfortunately, they help direct what actions we will and will not take.

I found it worthwhile to examine many of my Assessments or beliefs that shaped me as a young man. My thinking about my abilities and gifts, my age—especially now that I am eighty-six, how much money I need to be successful, race, religion, physical appearance, health, and in my youth, sex.

What are the ungrounded Truths that dominate and influence your life today?

Assertions. An Assertion is a statement you make for which you are willing to provide evidence. For example, suppose I say it's 72°F in this room. In that case, I will show you a thermometer that shows the temperature, and provided we agree the thermometer is accurate, I have asserted a fact.

Societies build specific ways of establishing and asserting common, often quantitative, values: weight, length, height, time, IQ, and so forth. These measurements, or Assertions, live as facts. Assertions are either true or false.

Remember, Assessments, different than Assertions, are neither true nor false. They are simply interpretations and opinions.

If you make an Assertion or a statement that is contrary to or ignores the evidence, you are mistaken or lying. You may have to withdraw the Assertion if you cannot provide proof.

Requests. A Request is an action you take to seek the assistance of another in satisfying an underlying concern. You want something, and you are asking something of another. A Request is made in the present, the moment you say it, but it invites a future action by another or others.

A Request also involves a commitment on the part of the requester to be satisfied. If the requester's conditions are met and the requester is unhappy, the person fulfilling the Promise (see below) may see the requester as manipulative, unfair, or demanding.

The performer might say of the requester, "They're jerking me around. First, they ask for something, and then when I do it, they're not satisfied!" What mood would such an experience produce in you? In me, it creates frustration and anger.

If the requester's conditions are clear to the performer and the conditions are not met, the requester may see the performer as unreliable or incompetent and begin to distrust them.

Offers. An Offer is the reverse of a Request. The requester may not know that another approach to satisfy a concern is available. The Offer is shared by the performer in the attitude of being of service to solve a problem. It is willingly made available to the requester for their consideration. In some circumstances, the Offer requires an expectation of acceptance and payment for the service. If it's just a conversation of ideas, it could be considered a gift. If the Offer requires service, a clear conversation regarding deliverables is needed so the requester knows what they are getting.

Promises. A Promise is when the performer speaks to indicate their commitment to fulfilling what someone else has requested. A Promise implies the performer fully understands the Request and is competent and sincere about fulfilling it. A Promise must include a date and time to be effectively managed.

The Importance of Trust

While not a Linguistic Act, I include Trust here because for these Linguistic Acts to function well, the fundamental social action of Trust is essential. Trust is a critical judgment about someone's rigor and sincerity as a promiser. When Promises are not fulfilled, and a person fails to take care of the consequences of the failure, the requester may feel betrayed or resentful and begin to distrust that particular promiser.

Trust lives in our Assessment of another's sincerity, ability, and responsibility to keep their Promises and commitments. Without Trust, relationships, organizations, and societies are in constant vigilance and chaos.

Communication Failures Cause Havoc

The fundamental challenge of relationships is guaranteed to produce miscommunication. Conflict generally results from the failure to listen.

Communication in language between two people is communication between two biological beings living in different cognitive universes. When we speak to another person, their system is triggered in unique ways that differ from how we would be triggered. When we speak, we are joining two worlds. Think of talking to your manager during a performance review, a teenage offspring about household chores, or a spouse while planning a vacation, and you can see what is meant by the perspective of two different worlds. Two worlds can collide.

Let me take you through the Conversation for Action and Results model so you can see how these distinctions help bring clarity and focused direction. To begin a Conversation for Action, the requester makes an Assessment that something is missing. They make a Declaration to correct the situation.

A Declaration is made at the beginning that something needs to be done and at the end when a Declaration of Satisfaction is made that the action solved the problem. When striking an agreement to provide service, it's helpful, and in many cases critical, that this requester has the authority to make the Request and to Declare their satisfaction with the results.

Assessment: Something is missing!

Missing Piece (Assessment)

The second action for the requester is to prepare an explicit Request. This model works best for coordinating action with employees within a business and between a business and their vendors. It also works well for families wanting to coordinate action effectively between parents and children.

Many supervisors or people with authority miss the boat in this area. They don't prepare an explicit Request and are disappointed and surprised when they don't get what they thought they requested. An explicit Request includes the date and time the performer will deliver the product or service as well as the conditions of satisfaction. Without a date it's very difficult, if not impossible at times, to manage a broken Promise.

Conversations for Results/Action (Promise Management)

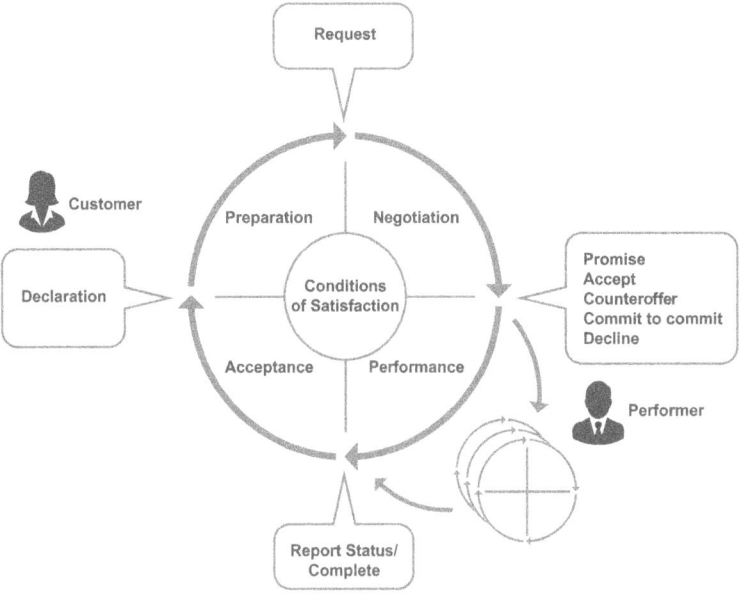

The original Conversations for Action graphic was created by Dr. Fernando Flores. The graphic above is an interpretation of his work.

The Performer (Negotiation)

The performer listening to the request negotiates the performance. The performer can make four promises:

1. They can accept the request, implying they are competent to fulfill it.
2. They may counteroffer, saying, "I can't do what you request, but I can offer this instead."
3. They could commit to commit, saying, "I'm not sure if I can do that; let me check with someone who knows and get back to you," with a date and time.

4. They could decline, saying, "No, I can't do that." For this negotiation to work successfully, *no* has to be recognized as a legitimate response. I've asked many people if they would rather have a *no* they can count on or a *yes* they can't. Most people recognize the *no* is the better answer because they can make other adjustments, such as asking an alternate person if the first one they've asked isn't going to do the work.

Here are key breakdowns I've witnessed in Promise Management:

1. The requester (such as a customer or supervisor) doesn't prepare an explicit Request. They haven't checked the person's competence to fulfill the Request or haven't secured a Promise with a delivery day and time the service or product will be delivered.
2. The performer, eager to please the requester, makes a Promise to deliver a result without first checking with the people who must provide it. This last piece is significant because doing so gives the requester an accurate time the product or service will be delivered without stressing the people who will provide it.
3. The performer might feel it's not okay to say no to the boss or requester and, therefore, will take on the engagement without checking what's critical to deliver and how the request will be fulfilled.
4. Some performers do not realize it's okay to offer an alternative solution. It requires checking with the customer to make sure the alternative meets their needs. It's still important for the performer to provide a Promise with a day and time the service or product will be delivered.

Two more critical moves need to be made to fulfill the Promise:

1. Status Report or Completion of Request (on the part of the Performer). The performer is responsible for keeping the requester (customer or supervisor) informed. The requester should *not* have to track down the performer to determine the status of fulfilling the service or product (the Request).

2. Declaration of Acceptance (on the part of the Requester). The requester is responsible for informing the performer they are satisfied or unsatisfied with the service or product delivered (Assertions and Assessments). If they are not happy, they are responsible for clearly informing the performer of what's missing (Assessments) and making a new Request.

The Importance of Keeping Promises

Growing up, I was told by my parents how important it is to keep Promises, but I realized how important it was for my identity and well-being only after I learned about these linguistic distinctions.

I often ask people how they feel when a Promise is made to them and then broken. The responses have ranged from highly disappointed to angry.

Not keeping Promises can bring toxic energy into any relationship. However, there are certain times when it's impossible to keep a Promise. That's why I like the perspective of being accountable for *managing* Promises versus *keeping* Promises.

Consider: *When does reality shift? When the promise is made, or when the promise is fulfilled?*

In my experience, most people think reality shifts when the Promise is fulfilled. Actually, reality changes when a Promise is made. Expectations and reality change for both the requester and the performer at the time the Promise is made. For example, if you and I agree to meet at 8:00 a.m. tomorrow, we both begin to arrange to show up at 8:00 a.m. The making of the Promise has already shifted our reality and actions.

In the same scenario, if I know I can't make it at 8:00 a.m., when would you rather know about it? When I don't arrive on time, and you wait for me, not knowing whether I will show up, or should I let you know I would be late for our meeting now, so you can choose to do something else until I show up?

Linguistic Viruses

I like that Dr. Budd uses his knowledge of medicine to call the common failures of communication *Linguistic Viruses*. I could relate to how medical viruses affect a human's ability to function and how linguistic viruses have the same impact, but the virus in this case is a misuse of language.

As you read this list of Budd's descriptions of linguistic viruses, consider how you can benefit from knowing these common breakdowns. He says the breakdowns or viruses attack relationships, alter individuals' structures, and cause dissatisfaction, bad moods, and even ill health. Once we have learned what they are, we can more effectively listen to others, work with them, and coordinate effective actions between them and ourselves.

There are ten linguistic viruses:
1. Not making Requests
2. Living with uncommunicated expectations
3. Making unclear Requests

4. Not observing the mood of requesting
5. Promising even when you aren't clear what was expected
6. Not declining Requests
7. Breaking Promises without taking care: undermining Trust
8. Treating Assessments as the Truth or as Assertions (facts)
9. Making Assessments without rigorous grounding
10. Making fantasy Affirmations and Declarations

As you think about these linguistic viruses, consider how learning to recognize them could improve communication and results. Learning to see and distinguish linguistic breakdowns and viruses has enabled me to coordinate action more effectively between others and myself.

To help businesses improve their internal communications, I created surveys of the Linguistic Viruses to help employees identify where the primary breakdowns occurred for them. Then we focused on removing the viruses that caused them the most pain.

Learning to Manage Broken Promises

One of the most disappointing outcomes when trying to coordinate action with someone is when the Promise is broken, and the expectations aren't fulfilled. Promise-keeping becomes extremely important for creating a positive, trusting, fulfilling work environment. It becomes essential for us to learn how to create a Promise we can manage.

Negotiations for successful Promises need to include a specified a date and time when the Promise will be fulfilled.

If we have that information, we can speak to the person about a broken Promise in this way:

1. Assertion *(a fact)*. On this day, you Promised to provide the product/service at this time and of this quality.

2. Assertion *(a fact)*. That time has come and gone. The product/service doesn't perform as you claimed it would.

3. Assessment *(an interpretation and opinion)*. I assess that because the delivery isn't on time and the product/service doesn't perform as expected, my Trust in your ability to deliver a quality item on time has diminished. I would like to have a trusting relationship with you in the future.

4. I Request that you take the necessary action to fulfill your Promise now.

These distinctions of Drs. Budd and Flores have allowed me to observe myself and others in coordinating action more effectively. I've observed how people create their reality in language and how powerfully language coordinates action and creates results. The six linguistic distinctions and Dr. Fernando Flores's Conversation for Action model were highly impactful in many vital areas of my life.

Here is how these distinctions improved my life:

- They were potent catalysts for improving my performance at work.
- They were a foundation for me to coordinate action more effectively with others.
- They improved the quality and fulfillment of my business offers, and I created happier clients.

- They helped me improve my relationships with my wife and with my children.
- They allowed me to make changes in my job, which improved my performance.
- They enhanced my ability to manage my health.

CHAPTER SEVEN

Manage Moods and Emotions

As I've stated before, a critical lesson in my learning journey is that I'm accountable and responsible for what I create in my life, which means I'm accountable and responsible for my moods and emotions. I believe my moods and emotions are predispositions for the action I take and the results I create.

It's important to differentiate between what is an *emotion* and what is a *mood*. The way I've learned to look at *emotions* is that they are triggered events. Something happens, and you don't have time to think about it. You react. If you get frightened and are afraid, a burst of anger may be the emotion you'll express, but it's only momentary.

A *mood* is something that lingers over a period of time. Like the day's mood, for instance: *Thank God it's Friday*. Cities have moods. If you ask a group of people what's the mood of San Francisco, they'll have an idea, or the mood of New York, the mood of New Orleans, the mood of Paris or any major city. Moods have a significant effect on your productivity in terms of opening you up to what you can get done on that day.

Let me give you an example. When we're depressed, overwhelmed, discouraged, or sad, it's hard to say: *It's a lovely day today*. When we're depressed, it's tough to take positive action. The converse is true also. If you're feeling good and you find it to be a beautiful day, it's hard to say: *Life sucks*. Taking positive action when you're in a good mood is much easier.

I know that I'm a lot better off if I act in a mood of being grateful than if I try to act from a mood of being sad, disappointed, or discouraged. And it's important to understand that what we say significantly impacts our moods.

In my learning journey, I've learned many lessons about the value of managing my mood.

Techniques for Mood Management

My first exposure to the concept of managing my mood came from reading *Psycho-Cybernetics* by Maxwell Maltz. It describes a cognitive behavioral and visualization technique to attain personal goals. This seminal, bestselling book has reportedly informed the work of athletic coaches in golf, basketball, and baseball as well as contemporary self-help experts such as Tony Robbins and Zig Ziglar.

From it, I learned you can't think a negative and a positive thought at the same time. When I realized I could choose to have a positive or a negative attitude, I thought: *Why not have a positive attitude? Then, I'll be more likely to get some good things done.* One comment that stands out for me is: *Attitude is everything, so why not pick a good one?*

My second exposure was in Lifespring workshops. That was the first time I experientially learned that I am accountable and responsible for what I create. The lesson on accountability solidly registered in me due to this workshop.

Newfield was my third exposure to ideas to manage my mood and emotions. Here's where I learned that we create our reality in language. Learning the distinctions of Linguistic Acts—like Declarations, Assessments, Assertions, Requests, Offers, and Promises—clarified how I could use language more effectively. It's been beneficial to understand the differences between Assessments and Assertions and realize my negative Assessments could lead to some poor moods. In addition, I discovered that broken Promises definitely affect my mood. Our moods affect our ability to listen, make and receive requests, and manage Promises.

Attending the Strozzi Institute was my fourth encounter in learning to manage moods and emotions. I learned they are held in my body and that I could learn how to leverage an emotional grab, find my center, and shift my perspective.

Reading *The Oz Principle* provided my fifth exposure. This book gave me a different interpretation of Accountability that has worked well for me and enabled me to manage my promises more effectively. It taught me how to recognize whether people were victims or living accountably and responsibly for what they create by how they talk.

My sixth exposure came from hearing what's been commonly, but erroneously, attributed to a Cherokee Grandfather's tale. There are many versions of this little story that reinforce the idea that negative and positive thoughts or moods constantly roll around in my head. The Grandfather describes our thoughts as wolves living inside us, fighting each other for survival. One wolf is evil and destructive, and the other is beneficial and kind. When his grandchild asks which wolf wins, the grandfather says, "The wolf that wins is the one that we feed the most."

Byron Katie, in her book *The Work* was my seventh exposure. *Finally*, I thought: *a book that provides me a way to shift my mood when I am trying to solve a particular problem.* Byron Katie's probing questions often open up another perspective so the stuck person can move on. She has one of the best processes for handling moods I've experienced. You can go to Byron Katie's website, thework.com, and find that she has two pages listing emotions and moods. You can choose which mood you're in at a particular time.

My eighth exposure continues to be provided by Shirzad Chamine. In his mental fitness coach training program and his book *Positive Intelligence* (Greenleaf Book Group Press, 2012), Shirzad points out that our Judge and Saboteurs have controlled our lives and moods since birth. He teaches a process in which I'm learning how to catch my Judge and Saboteurs in action and reduce their impact on my ability to create my effective results. His process also teaches me to improve the effectiveness of my Sage, both in thinking about and in solving my Saboteur issues.

Another resource that I've recently come across is the work of Marcus Aurelius, an Emperor of the Roman Empire from 161 CE to his death in 180 CE. His writings on emotional Stoicism are in books called *Meditations*. He understood a lot about moods way back in history.

Here are a few quotes that are widely attributed to Aurelius, although whether he actually wrote them remains a bit of a mystery—certainly the ideas are consistent with his writing:

- "You have power over your mind — not outside events. Realize this, and you will find strength."
- "The happiness of your life depends upon the quality of your thoughts."

- "Everything we hear is an opinion, not a fact. Everything we see is a perspective, not the truth."

Managing My Mood

For the last seven years I've been managing my mood with a practice I call *Blessings,* a take-off from Shawn Achor's model of recording three gratitudes daily to help change one's mood—one of five options of a twenty-one-day challenge to adopt a new habit in order to rewire the brain for happiness. He introduced these options during his TEDx talk, "The Happy Secret to Better Work."

The discipline of recording blessings daily works well for me. Blessings, as I define them, are sights, circumstances, or events over which I have no control, such as blue sky, sunshine, rain, rivers, lakes, ice, snow, trees, bushes, birds, bird songs, flowers, animals, dogs, cats, horses, squirrels, rabbits, bears, lions, fish—and so on. And the list can be expanded by the different kinds of trees, flowers, birds, and bird songs. For example, some sources report there are more than 300 horse breeds in the world. Noting Blessings is my way of acknowledging my higher power's involvement in my life.

My goal is to observe ten blessings a day, and I share my blessings with five other people. That way, not only do I get my blessings for the day, but I also get to see their blessings. On a good day, when everyone shares, I experience sixty blessings. This practice has done wonders in helping me maintain a positive mood.

Here's another way to look at managing moods:

- If you Oppose the Fact of Life, you can feel a mood of Resentment.

- If you Oppose the Possibilities, you can feel a mood of Resignation.
- If you Accept the Fact of Life, you can feel a mood of Acceptance and Peace
- If you Accept the Possibilities, you can feel a mood of Energy and Ambition.

Moods and Action

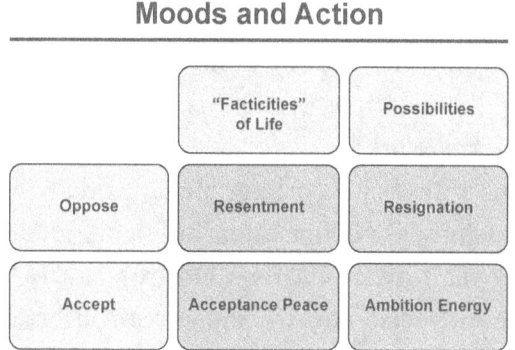

Moods, Emotions, and Actions

Moods and emotions determine what we can and cannot achieve in work, learning, relationships, and so on. Emotions and moods are predispositions for action. Our emotional life is crucial in every sphere of human action. For example, the possibilities of coordinating action with a colleague are narrowed in a mood of distrust. But in a mood of excitement, our horizon of possible actions is expanded for future activities.

According to our mood, some actions are possible, and others are not; some possibilities are opened, and others are closed.

Moods are not specific, and we usually cannot relate them to particular events. Moods live in the background of our actions. Moods start as emotions, and they become moods if the feeling stays long enough with us.

Moods are perceivable outside individual experiences as well. Different places have different moods. Time cycles also bring different moods. Different ages are also associated with different moods.

Emotions are always bound to particular events; we can typically point to the circumstances that generate them. They are specific and reactive. Events precede them.

Moods and Conversations

According to our moods, our conversations are different. We speak and listen differently. One of the problems we face is that moods are often invisible to us. We don't notice the moods and assume that what belongs to our moods are properties of our world.

We usually assume that the world *is* how we perceive it; we don't typically see the negative and positive features of the world resulting from the mood we are in.

What can we do about moods?

Moods are the way we're looking at the world. Often, we become so powerless to change our moods, we don't take responsibility for the moods we create. We can actually modify our attitudes (or beliefs), thereby changing our horizon of possibilities.

We have the power to change our horizon of possibilities through conversations and through being in moods of exploration and innovation. Conversations can be powerful tools for designing moods.

Guidelines for Design

Moods and emotions are with us much of the time. Learning to work with them rather than ignoring them or pretending they don't exist can enhance both personal and business worlds. This is accomplished first by becoming an observer of our moods—learning to identify them as moods and not as how things are.

Beware of the stories we have built around our moods. Often the mood creates the story. Examine underlying Assertions and Assessments. Are the Assessments grounded or ungrounded?

Don't forget the connection between our bodies and our moods. Ultimately, we cannot avoid moods, but we can manage them.

The person accountable for managing my mood is me. Emotions are triggered events and can dissipate quickly, but if I dwell on the experience, it can become a mood. Moods linger. I can create better results from a positive mood than a negative one. The moods that are in control of me are the ones I feed the most.

Blessings—the practice of recording what I'm grateful for each day—has been an excellent way to manage my mood. Blessings enable me to celebrate all the things that come to me that I don't have any control over and create a positive mood. In addition, through Positive Intelligent exercises, I can reduce the impact of my Judge and Saboteurs on my mood and performance and free myself up to make better Sage choices.

CHAPTER EIGHT

Values Make a Critical Difference

I thought I had mastered the process of being happy and fulfilled in my work when I learned the secret to being successful in my life was to find my natural gifts and talents, be creative in them, and then implement my creations. It's the foundation by which I chose to live my life.

That is, until I shared my discovery with a gifted life coach named Richard Leider after one of his many presentations that I attended. I shared with him my life-planning experience with the book *Where Do I Go from Here With My Life*, written by Crystal and Bolles. Richard Leider had personally met Richard Bolles and was very familiar with his work.

Richard Leider said to me, "You're right. It's important to creatively capitalize on your natural gifts and talents, but you're missing a critical thing."

"What's that?"

"Values. It's important that you're working on something, or in some place, where your values line up."

Thanks to Richard, this concept became an essential addition to my life plan: *To creatively capitalize on my natural gifts and talents by implementing my creations, where I choose to be of service, and where my values line up.*

As I've coached people, I've found people enjoying their work, but if they were working in a situation where their values didn't align, they were unhappy. Eventually, they would leave the role that was causing them pain.

In Richard Leider's workshop, he has a value selection process. I've refined his list to work for me.

Here are my Top Eleven Values—with a few subheadings—in the ranked order I've chosen to live my life by, along with my rationale.

1. *Inner Harmony.* Possessing a strong sense of personal peace as well as freedom from inner conflict and guilt. My chosen Driving Life Force is to live my life with Peace, Joy, and Serenity.

   a. *Accountability.* Lifespring stressed the idea of keeping commitments, which I liked, but I really like the terminology of Accountability and Managing Promises in the book *The Oz Principle*, discussed in more detail in Chapter Three.

   b. *Integrity.* I knew from my parents how important it was to keep promises and to tell the truth, but I never embodied this thought like I currently do until, and after, I took the Basic Lifespring course.

2. *Pleasure.* Living with an attitude of gratitude, joy, and happiness. Being happy and having fun; an enjoyable, pleasurable lifestyle. For years I've heard about the

concept of living with an "attitude of gratitude," and I do, but I have a much better feeling when I'm celebrating what I call *Blessings*, the daily practice of recording what I'm grateful for.

3. *Wisdom.* A developed, mature understanding of life and people used to enlighten and guide others. Through my goals of being a lifelong learner and my desire to creatively capitalize on my natural gifts and talents wherever they take me, I've come to believe "the more I know, the more I know I don't know." This approach to learning has made my life more interesting and exciting. One of the joys, as well as frustrations, I've had in writing this book is confirming what I've learned and learning what I haven't learned yet. It's really been a wonderful, exploratory journey.

4. *Health.* Being able to maintain well-being. My definition of well-being includes physical, mental, and emotional well-being, as well as play. This may be a strange list of things I think are essential to health. I developed the list over time based on my life experiences.

    a. *Physical Health.* Right now, my wife and I are experiencing issues with arthritis—something neither of us expected to deal with at this stage in our lives. We're still looking for ways to manage the pain effectively. It's affected both our mental and emotional spirit.

    b. *Mental Health.* When you experience good mental health, you're more expansive in what you can do, and it's easier to manage your mindset to be optimistic about life. I genuinely believe that my moods and emotions are predispositions for the action. I also think I'm accountable and responsible for managing my moods and emotions. Byron Katie's work is especially helpful in exploring mental health.

c. *Spiritual Health.* Pursuing spiritual values, knowledge, and experiences is possible when we are in good spiritual health. Because of my upbringing in an evangelist religion, I've struggled with not seeing spiritual health as a religious effort. My Blessings practice brings me peace and acceptance that there is something greater than myself making things happen. This approach has enabled me to leave humans' dogma, rules, and regulations behind. Using the linguistic distinctions of Assessments (which are interpretations and opinions) and Assertions (which are facts) from Fernando Flores's work has brought me additional clarity and appreciation of the gifts of life that I've been given.

d. *Play.* For the longest time, I never felt that play was important to my health, but as I've become older, I've realized it is imperative to balance my life between working hard and having joy, peace, and serenity. While I enjoy what I do for work, I know it's important for me to play and to enjoy it also. I've learned that if I don't take care of myself, it's hard, if almost impossible, for me to take care of others, which is the reason that Health is before Family in my list of values.

e. *Family.* Meeting family members' relational, emotional, and, if needed, financial needs. I learned this lesson powerfully in the psych ward after my wife's death. I learned from the therapy nurse that I was *always at choice* regarding how I wanted to take care of my four children without a partner to help share the load.

5. *Mature Love.* Cultivating mutual affection and emotional, sexual, and spiritual intimacy with my lifelong partner, applying lessons I learned primarily from Onsite.

6. *Independence.* I maintain a self-reliant, self-sufficient attitude toward my work and life. Determining the nature of my work without significant direction from others is crucial for me to be at choice regarding what I would like to work on, where I would like to contribute, and with whom I would like to work. Working interdependently with others is very important to me to accomplish business objectives. I've had to learn to be adaptable to and flexible within the situations I've experienced, and I've learned to trust and apply my creativity and innovation to solve problems. This path has been very satisfying and rewarding for me.

a. Time Freedom. Having work responsibilities that I can pursue according to my schedule. No specific work hours are required.

b. Adaptability, Flexibility, Creativity, Innovation. Being oriented toward imaginative, creative, or pioneering types of work.

c.   Freedom to Choose: how I spend my time without worrying about creating income.

7.   *Leadership.* Opportunity to influence, direct, and inspire others to accomplish chosen tasks. Patrick Lencioni's book *The 6 Types of Working Genius* (Matt Holt Books, 2022) offers another way to understand the skills you and your team have, as well as understanding frustrations that can arise. I've learned that I have the gifts of *wonder* and *enablement.* Recently I learned that Patrick Lencioni believes wonder indicates a need for improvement or change, and enablement can initiate support and can aide the implementation of the idea or solution. I always wondered why I wasn't inspired to be the CEO of a large organization. The information from Lencioni has given me peace. I get a lot of fulfilment out of supporting and assisting individuals in their growth and helping them implement their ideas and solutions.

8.   *Sense of Accomplishment.* Making a lasting contribution that others and I recognize and appreciate as worthwhile. I need to accomplish goals. This clarity came from *Psycho-Cybernetics.* In the book, author Maxwell Maltz points out that we humans are goal-seeking beings— even the goal of not having a goal is a goal. I've also come to appreciate how important it is that what I work on is recognized and appreciated as worthwhile. Not everything I've worked on has turned out to be worthwhile, so I'm more selective now.

9. *Mental Stimulation.* Work that requires constantly using one's mind to continue to develop one's intellect. Wow—how significant this value is to me! I see myself as a lifelong learner. I'm aware that the more I know, the more I don't know, which is exciting for me. Being a lifelong learner has kept my life fascinating and frustrating at times. To be a true learner, you must start as a beginner. Beginners make a lot of mistakes until they learn enough to be competent and proficient. I've had to learn how to accept my failures and mistakes and zigzag to success by learning from my failures and mistakes. It's been important to give myself the patience to understand, learn, and accept my lack of competence as I continue to learn and grow.

10. *Location.* Living where one most wants to live or where it best suits one's lifestyle. After all the traveling I did during the early part of my career and the many places I've had the opportunity to visit, we've chosen to live in Chippewa Falls, Wisconsin, on a lake. I love Wisconsin in the summertime, but I don't enjoy the cold winter weather. Last week, it was -8°F with a windchill of -31°F. Too cold for me. For eighteen years, my wife and I lived seven months in Wisconsin and the five winter months in Arizona, until I contracted Valley Fever—a fungal infection caused by Coccidioides organisms. I've chosen not to expose myself to that possibility again. Covid and arthritis have limited our travel choices, but we're hopeful that the opportunity to travel freely will return.

11. *Stability, including financial stability.* At this stage in our lives, my life partner and I feel very fortunate to be financially secure with minimum change or variety necessary. I believe some variety is essential, so I've chosen to write this book, hired a writing coach, and re-joined Toastmasters to be involved in meaningful conversations and practice public speaking. I'll be exploring what other ideas might be fulfilling.

What Are Your Core Values?

Finding my Core Values became very important to me, and they have guided me through more than half my life. My Core Values were also an aid in helping me choose my purpose. From my experience, I can say it's well worth the effort to explore and find your Core Values.

CHAPTER NINE

Involve Your Body in Learning

When I first started learning about Ontological Coaching with Julio Olalla and Rafael Echeverria from Newfield Network, I was intrigued by their three ways to intervene in a client's story and coach them:

1. Language: people spin their stories so fast
2. Emotions: an excellent way to access stuck points
3. Body: the body is all-knowing and holds some of the stuck points until they are released

I thought they did an excellent job teaching Language and Emotions, but I didn't connect with how they taught the coaching method through the Body. I met the person who had initially connected me with Newfield, and he looked different. I asked him what the difference was, and he said it was the training he'd been receiving from Richard Strozzi-Heckler at Strozzi Institute.

When I signed up for the initial training in Petaluma, California, where the dojo is, I intended to find another *coaching arrow* to put into my quiver of coaching methods. What I found was the quiver that held all the coaching arrows.

Several body training exercises, I recall, had a significant impact on my life. The training was based on the martial art of Aikido, which I found impressive. I'd never considered learning martial arts before and was unaware of Aikido.

I learned a tremendous amount about my body in the dojo:

1. *Centering.* I learned how to find my center and remain balanced while standing, sitting, and walking. I still use this method of finding and operating from my balanced center today. For me, this exercise continues to feel very powerful. It's amazing how powerful one can be operating from their balanced center.

2. *Releasing tension in my body.* As we walked around the dojo, one of the instructors constantly reminded me to relax my jaw, which was always tense. My jaw was a good reminder that I was carrying stress, and I could release it.

3. *The Grab.* What a revelation this exercise was! I didn't realize how my body reacted to a negative comment or experience. We would practice telling someone something they shared that would trigger them. The learning was to experience how that grab felt in our bodies when we heard the comment. Then we would breathe, find our center, set an intention, face the grab, and, from the center, take forceful action. I still use and teach this today.

4. *The Jo.* The Jo is the stick the warriors learned to use in combat. The Jo kata we learned had thirty-two moves. It revealed what was happening in my life and gave me new ideas when I struggled with learning. When I experienced a part of the jo kata where I would get stuck or fail, I learned to relax, take a deep breath, and slowly practice the move until I could do it fluently. When I had trouble learning, my body could guide me to be more relaxed and accepting with this powerful learning experience. By taking on this new mental approach, I could address the steps I was learning more successfully.

5. *The Randori.* The learning was modeled to use the moves of Aikido to help us experience options in our bodies to address breakdowns and confrontations we encounter in our daily lives. I can't remember the various Aikido moves today, but the ones we learned were beneficial. In this exercise, the class of sixty people arranges themselves in a circle around an individual in the center. *Randori* is a "random attack," and class members take turns walking directly toward the center individual with their hands outstretched, as if they were going for the throat. When it was my turn in the middle, my role was to use the various Aikido moves I'd been taught to ward off the extended arms. As the nine-month training progressed, the moves got faster and more intense, and our skills advanced. This modeled what was happening in my life personally and in business. With the somatic skills I'd learned,

I realized I was at choice; that is, I could choose to stand and be hit, to deflect, or to turn around the issues I couldn't handle at that time.

6. *The Two-Step.* By doing the two steps in Aikido, I could learn when I was centered and balanced. I could do the two-step movement by myself, from both directions, and improve my ability to move from a centered position. I could also do the two-step with another person, which is like a ballet when you're moving in step with another person. With some of the two-step exercises, we visualized specific images. The one that impacted me the most was doing the two-step with an image of a giant dinosaur tail attached to me. For me, it was trying to move while swinging my past life and beliefs with me. It was much easier to let my past life and limiting beliefs go.

The fantastic parts of the learning were how much my body was involved in the learning process and how it could tell me where I was in the process. This knowledge would have been valuable for me in high school and college.

I still use many of these exercises for myself and my clients today. I found feeling emotions and centering in my body particularly useful when I did equine-assisted coaching with horses. The horses give me instant feedback on emotions that I or my client might be harboring at the time. I found it almost impossible to get the horse to move to my request if I wasn't making the request from my center and my power.

CHAPTER TEN

Accept Loss and Deal With Grief

For years, I have felt that we, as a society, have done a poor job preparing children, teenagers, and grown-ups to successfully deal with significant losses in their lives and the resulting grief. There is an opportunity for us all to learn how best to honor what we've lost, accept that it's gone, choose to let go, and move on to what is next for us in our lives.

I believe, in real time, our lives are very short, so we're at choice regarding how much time we spend grieving and how much time we spend getting on with our lives.

We experience loss and disappointment differently from one another. Grieving is a highly individualized process. No "one approach fits all" applies here. Adapting to a significant loss varies dramatically from one person to another. It often depends on a person's history, beliefs, and knowledge of dealing with significant losses as well as to their relationship with what was lost.

Learning as children how to deal with loss is helpful and useful. The loss could be of something like a toy or a doll, or of something greater, like a pet, friend, sibling, or parent.

Our grief is not limited to feelings of sadness. Losing a loved one can encompass a range of feelings and several emotions that live in our bodies, from deep sadness and sorrow to anger, resentment, regrets, or feeling like a victim. Feeling many different emotions is customary in the grieving process. The important lesson is to get in touch with where in our bodies we feel our losses and how to deal with these feelings so we can release them.

After Shirley's untimely death, I attended multiple workshops regarding grief and read some beneficial books like:

- *On Death and Dying* (Tavistock Publications, 1970) by Elisabeth Kubler-Ross
- *Transitions: Making Sense of Life's Changes* (Addison-Wesley Publishing Comp, 1981) by William Bridges
- *The Way* of *Transition: Embracing Life's Most Difficult Moments* (Da Capo Press, 2001) by William Bridges
- *Grief Counselling and Grief Therapy: A Handbook for the Mental Health Practitioner, Fourth Edition* (Springer Publishing Company, 2018) by J. William Worden

Worden conceptualizes grief to be a series of four tasks:
1. To accept the reality of the loss
2. To work through the pain of grief
3. To adjust to an environment in which the deceased is missing
4. To relocate and memorialize the loved one

In researching this chapter of my book, I've found a lot of good information about dealing with loss and grief available on the internet, in other books, and in workshops. There are also people who are certified in Grief Recovery to help guide you through the process.

A book called *Grief Recovery Handbook: 20th Anniversary Expanded Edition – The Action Program for Moving Beyond Death, Divorce, and Other Losses, Including Health, Career, and Faith* by John W. James and Russell Friedman (William Murrow Paperbacks, 2017) is one that really resonates with me. The authors have created a group that, among other things, certifies Grief Recovery practitioners to enable them to use specific processes that help people overcome grief, including trauma and PTSD.

Some losses we experience as adults are more severe and affect us more deeply than others; for example, the loss of a loved one (child, mate, parent, sibling, friend, pet), or the loss of something especially important, like a part of our physical body, our sight, our hearing, our overall health, a job, a career, or a position. Some of these losses are so impactful that when they occur, we are stopped in our tracks.

As I'm writing this, I realize I'm primarily talking about the attitudes of people in Western cultures toward significant losses such as death and divorce. Death and divorce are often depicted as circumstances to fight or resist. People in Eastern cultures tend to characterize death as a part of life. In Eastern cultures, death is often considered more of a transition than an end. People in death-denying cultures tend to have more anxiety about death than people in death-accepting cultures.

For us in Western culture, the emotion of grief can expand to involve guilt, yearning, anger, and, for some, a sense of being a victim of circumstances. Grief can be very confusing. One may find themselves grieving the loss of a painful relationship. Another might mourn the loss of a loved one who died from cancer while also feeling relieved the person is no longer suffering. These grief emotions are surprising in their strength, and they can be challenging to release.

The most complex challenge I've experienced in my life was accepting loss and adjusting to living a new reality without the presence of my loved partner. Letting go and moving on was a huge challenge. Life is not a dress rehearsal, and I don't have an opportunity for do-overs. Life is very short. I either *use it or lose it*. While living to eighty-six may seem like a long time in our current lifespan, it isn't very long in the scope of how long humanity has existed. I realize the faster I can choose to accept the situation, the faster I can choose to let it go and decide what's next for me.

This drawing, called "The Whirlpool of Grief," made available by Dr. Richard Wilson, is the best depiction of dealing with grief I've encountered.

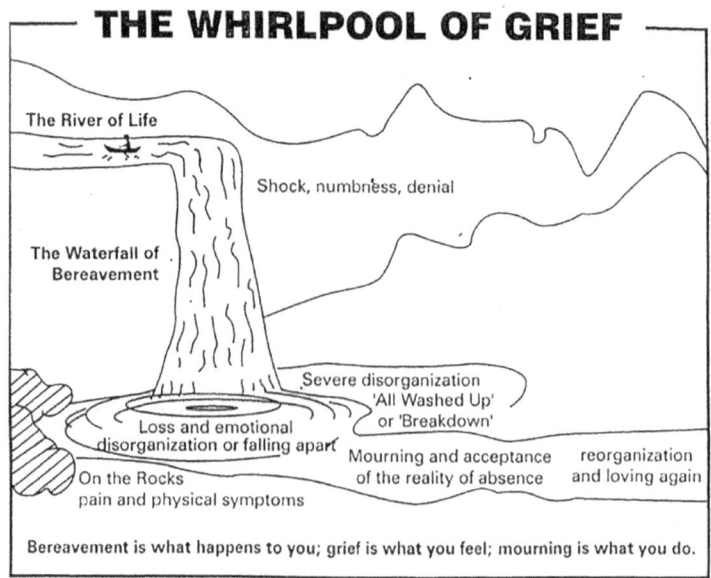

THE WHIRLPOOL OF GRIEF

The River of Life

Shock, numbness, denial

The Waterfall of Bereavement

Severe disorganization 'All Washed Up' or 'Breakdown'

Loss and emotional disorganization or falling apart

Mourning and acceptance of the reality of absence

reorganization and loving again

On the Rocks pain and physical symptoms

Bereavement is what happens to you; grief is what you feel; mourning is what you do.

This drawing depicts very well the experiences I've had grieving the significant losses in my life, like the loss of my wife in 1979, the loss of my job in a company I'd worked in for more than eighteen years, and the loss of other relationships.

As I reflect on the grief work that I've done, I've learned that unresolved loss and grief have been significant barriers to achieving my goals. Through my persistence, I found several ways to deal with my deep losses and grief and to let them go, so I could move forward. Being able to write this book is one example of my dealing with a loss and grief that got freed up because of the work I did. I let go of a longtime negative experience that I have been sad about and grieved for many years.

My personal experiences of dealing with loss and grief are why I think it's so essential for all of us to develop a basic understanding of how to overcome loss and grief, especially as we get older. As we get older, we have even more losses. More relatives, friends, and classmates pass away. We also experience the loss of our own health with diseases like cancer, heart attacks, strokes, arthritis, loss of limbs, rotator cuff tears, hip replacements, macular degeneration, and concussions from falling, to name a few others.

Based on my learning to *be the observer of the observer I am*, I've realized that most of what I'd learned about dealing with grief was from the people at the church I attended as a child and my wife's family when she passed.

My History of Major Losses and Grief
My initial experience dealing with death was when a grade school friend drowned at the age of seven. I didn't have a clue what to do at the funeral or how to process my sadness that

my favorite friend was no longer in my life. At that time, there weren't any school grief counselors, and nothing was offered to help children deal with the loss of a friend.

My second significant experience with grief was my mother's journey with Guillain-Barré Syndrome. Our family didn't know whether she would recover and return home or remain sick and pass away in the hospital. She was the second identified case treated at the University of Minnesota, and they didn't know how to treat the disease then. My parents spent their last fifty dollars in savings to get my mother into the University test program. It took five years before she was ultimately released from the doctors' care. My father did the best he could working, dealing with his wife being in the hospital for six months, and raising three kids. As the eldest child, ten years old—my brother was nine; my sister was six—I did a lot of cooking for dinner, washing clothes, and cleaning the house during that time.

My third experience was during my first year of college, when my high school sweetheart left for Washington, D.C., to be an airline ticket agent. She promised she'd be back in six months to continue our relationship. Based on her promise, I signed up for eight years in the Air Force Reserves. I mistakenly thought our relationship was so strong we would get married. The truth is I never saw her again.

When my wife, Shirley, passed away, my experience with how to deal with deep grieving mainly came from her family. Shirley died ten months after she was diagnosed with leukemia. During her illness, the primary way of looking for healing and recovery was working with the medical community, reading clinical medical papers, and praying. When Shirley passed, family members, friends, and church members attended her funeral. Praying and crying were the primary ways they dealt with the loss, but no one had suggestions for ways to overcome grief in the long term.

After reading James and Friedman's work, *The Grief Recovery Handbook* (Collins, 2009), I wondered: *Where did people learn how to deal with loss and grief?* My answer: *From their parents and the people at their church.*

I didn't realize how many limiting beliefs I had adopted over my forty years regarding how to deal with grief and loss and how my beliefs were affecting my relationships. After Shirley's death, I struggled for fifteen years, attempting to put together a healthy, loving relationship with a woman who would serve us both as well as our children.

The way I finally solved this dilemma was to go for my fifty-fifth birthday to Onsite Workshops which, at the time, were in Rapid City, South Dakota.

Letting Go Through a Psychodrama Experience

Psychodrama is a structured form of therapy in which a person dramatizes a personal problem or conflict, usually in front of a group of other therapy participants. The other participants usually take part in the drama, though each performance focuses on a single person's concerns. For instance, someone might re-enact a troubling scene from the past with others playing roles of various individuals involved.

In what I would call a *psychodrama experience*, I discovered I had deep anger toward the church regarding my mother's illness when I was ten and when my wife died of leukemia.

In the psychodrama workshop session, based on the information I shared, the therapist created a Freeborg family scene that reenacted the day after a childhood Christmas, when my mother was in the hospital. My brother, sister, and I were standing outside the hospital in the cold of winter, outfitted with our Christmas gifts. We kids were looking up to the third floor of the hospital to see my mother, who had been there for several months.

The psychodrama group member who portrayed my mother stood on a chair with a sheet across half her face and body. The other participants, who portrayed my brother, my sister, and me, were all on their knees, looking up to the imaginary third floor to see my mother.

As kids, we were thrilled to see our mother. Our mother was delighted to see us. At that time in history, hospitals didn't allow children to see patients in the hospital. Because of the depression my mother was experiencing and the fact that it was the day after Christmas, the nursing staff had arranged to make an exception for my mother and our family, and they snuck us kids into the hospital.

While I was standing back, reflecting, and looking over the scene the therapist had created, the therapist asked someone in the group to put their hands on the shoulders of the young boy portraying me and apply pressure and push down on the shoulders. Watching this felt very real to me.

"How does this scene feel to you?" asked the therapist.

I said, "It feels very familiar. That's what it felt like when I was home taking care of my brother and sister when my mom was in the hospital. I felt a lot of pressure and responsibility."

The therapist then asked, "Where does someone ten years old go for help when his dad is working, his mom is in the hospital, and he's busy taking care of his brother and sister?"

I was quiet for a moment. "Would he go to his dad?" asked the therapist.

I said, "I've already dealt with my anger issues toward my father at Lifespring. That's not the issue here."

The therapist then said, "How about relatives? Neighbors? The Church?"

"Fuck the church!" I said, remembering all the praying that had gone on when my mom and wife were sick, and the praying when my wife died. Even though everyone prayed, my wife died.

The therapist leveraged my angry outburst and immediately engaged me in anger release work with the group. I vigorously kicked pillows, swung, and hit chairs and cubes with a Bataka Encounter Bat. There was still more anger to release after all these efforts, so the therapist set up a tug-of-war between me and the group. It was five people on one end of the rope versus just me on the other. I would not give in. Finally, the therapist told the group to let me win.

I was exhausted after this experience. The therapist asked me to sit in a corner of the room, rest, and hug a little teddy bear. The scene was to represent the adult me giving comfort and support to the little boy me, represented by the teddy bear, while I was recovering from the anger of grieving. Several days after the workshop, I purchased a teddy bear that I still have today to remind me of this experience.

Putting together what had happened, I realized I had been living with unresolved grief trapped in my body from losses I'd experienced years ago—primarily the loss of my thirty-three-year-old mother's availability during her illness when I was ten years old, and the loss of my wife.

I realized I had developed a belief system that wasn't working for me. The belief I'd come up with was: *I can trust the women I love to leave me,* and I was creating that reality.

I'm happy to report that the combination of my new belief systems that I've adopted over the years are working for me:

1. I can trust the women I love to be with me forever. Not physically, but mentally. I think of them and feel their presence almost every day.

2. I am accountable and responsible for what I create in my life—my past and present.

3. I am living as an observer of the observer I am.

4. My body holds onto feelings of loss and grief. Releasing the long-held anger in my body regarding these losses freed me up to having my very loving relationship with my life partner for more than thirty years.

Other Ways of Letting Go and Moving On

Not every way to deal with loss and grief has to be as dramatic as I just portrayed. There are other ways to let go and move on.

Another successful way I've experienced dealing with profound loss, trauma, and PTSD is coaching and therapy with horses. See Chapter Twelve, "Let Horses Be Your Guide."

Today the questions I ask myself to get beyond significant losses and grief are:

- *What about this loss do I need to accept so I can move on?*
- *What do I have to let go of to begin creating my new future?*
- *Where in my body am I experiencing this loss?*
- *What do I have to do to release it?*
- *What do I wish to create during my one short life on this earth, knowing that, if I'm fortunate, I'll live another ten years?*
- *Why do I want to create it?*
- *What steps do I need to take to create it?*
- *If I'm still blocked or stuck, what resource will I use to gain clarity to move on?*

CHAPTER ELEVEN

Learn to Deal With Fear and Ask for Help

I experience fear as something that stops me from taking the action necessary to create something I desire. Most of the time, fear lives in my head, but it also lives in my throat and chest. Sometimes, when I've been really afraid, fear the size of a small volleyball has been in my stomach.

Over the years, I've encountered several approaches for dealing with fear effectively. Most of these lessons have come through experiential learning.

"Do the thing you fear the most, and the death of fear is certain," was the first advice I received about combating fear. It was given to me by an insurance salesman, Robert J. Gallivan, who had been very successful. He wrote the book *How I Started Earning $50,000 a Year in Sales at the Age of 26* (Prentiss Hall, 1963). I was impressed—it was a lot of money in 1966; adjusted for inflation, that's about $487,000 in 2024. So, I tried to follow his model.

While it's a great line and primarily true, it wasn't that helpful to me in dealing with fear.

Learning to Ask for Help

My first significant lesson regarding how to deal directly with fear occurred when my wife died at thirty-nine years of age from leukemia. I instantly became a widower with four young children. Two weeks after her funeral, I was directed to terminate ten people working in my department. Five months after the funeral, my job in a company I'd worked for over eighteen years was eliminated. It was in the middle of a recession. Unemployment was 10–12 percent, and interest rates were 18–20 percent. I was a widower with four young children, no wife to help raise them, no job, and no money. I was afraid. This was one of the first instances I learned the lessons to ask for help and that I was *always at choice*. You can read about how I started my recovery in the psych ward in Chapter One.

My next major lesson regarding how to deal with fear came from a course at Newfield Network with Julio Olalla. "Be an observer of the observer you are," Julio used to say at the beginning of his workshops. In other words, look at the results you're achieving and the actions you're taking to achieve them. I learned that most people, including myself at that time, keep trying to change their actions if they weren't getting the results they wanted.

When I struggled to achieve my goals, Julio taught me to examine my beliefs about taking action and creating the desired results. Then, I needed to explore whether my beliefs were helping or hindering my actions and results. I was looking at how I was looking at the world. I was being an observer of the observer I was.

If you're not accomplishing the desired results, analyze your fears and see how to address them. I've found this approach to be very helpful. I used this approach for my first trip to Australia and New Zealand. My consulting business was only seven months old when I made the trip. To prepare for the trip, I made a list of all my fears and came up with twenty-three reasons I shouldn't take it. I realized I would be fine if I dealt with the first three concerns. I went on the trip and had an outstanding experience.

My next big breakthrough in dealing with fear came from an Outward Bound experience in the White Mountains of Maine. In one of our exercises, we climbed a shear wall with a belayer—a partner below you as you climb, keeping tension on a rope tied to your harness. The idea is that they will slow your descent if you fall.

I did okay climbing up the wall. I struggled in several situations but did okay going up the wall overall. However, I freaked out when I was supposed to go back down.

I was asked to step off the cliff backward into space and trust that I would be okay being supported by the belayer and the belay line. The idea took my breath away.

It took me about forty minutes to get up enough nerve, courage, and trust to lean backward and step off the cliff. It felt like my heart skipped a beat when I did it. The Jumpmaster didn't believe it when I did it. His experience was that most people who wait that long don't take the plunge.

The combination of the wall climbing and the ropes course taught me another way to look at fear—as an acronym:

FEAR = False Expectations Appearing Real.

I learned I was safe because I had a belayer, a belay line, and a harness, but my fear of heights—or more accurately, my fear of falling and dying—limited me from taking action.

Fear = *False Expectations Appearing Real* has been a good mantra for me to remember, reflect on, and process when examining what I'm afraid of.

Additional ideas for dealing with fear come from a whitewater rafting trip with my son, Michael, in Costa Rica.

One Rapid at a Time

To celebrate Michael's graduation from college, I offered him a whitewater rafting opportunity in Costa Rica so we could have a bonding experience.

One thing that made the experience particularly challenging for me was that when I was Michael's age, I had flipped a canoe trying to shoot the rapids in the spring run-off at Taylors Falls, Minnesota. Once I was out of the canoe, the river kept tumbling me, pulling me under, giving me only seconds to capture a breath. I bobbed up and down several times and felt I was at death's doorstep. Fortunately, I survived the experience, but the memory is still very real to me. I've never forgotten how blessed I felt to have survived the river's forceful pull.

Even though I recently had been on an Outward Bound experience and had learned the difference between *real* and *imagined* fear, the idea of shooting rapids in a raft in a strange country for nine days created anxiety for me.

The first day went smoothly. We floated down the river and over some rapids, but nothing too tricky.

On the second day of our experience on the General River, we came upon a huge wave called *Chachalaca*. We made a left turn in the river, and there it was—a vast, monstrous wave that was eighteen feet high, or one-and-a-half stories tall, and twenty-three feet in circumference. It curled over like a colossal surfing wave.

Our river guide had advised us that rafts without enough momentum to get over the top of the wave would flip over, and people would be popped out of the raft into the heart of the wave like little toothpicks.

Our rafting team could not create enough momentum, and everyone in the raft was tossed out of the raft into the river like little toothpicks.

I came up underneath the raft floor, white air bubbles all around me, but no air to breathe. Initially, I was calm and struggled to hold onto my sandals. In a moment, I decided I was better off letting my sandals go and getting to the end of the raft where I could breathe. It seemed like it took forever, and some fear started to creep in. It felt like that time in Minnesota, when whitewater rapids were forcefully pulling me under the water, and I knew my life was in danger.

Eventually, I got out from under the raft and was rescued by a kayaker who took me safely to shore. That experience of shooting the rapids was enough for me that day, and I was okay with just paddling the raft to our following site.

The next day, I was flipped out of the raft at the first rapid. This time, I bumped my knee hard on a rock. After returning to the raft, I began to ponder my situation. I was safe now, but what was coming up next? I had been told there were some life-threatening class IV and class V rapids further down the river. I was getting anxious about the whole experience. I admit it; I was scared.

At the time, I didn't think my options were great. I could walk out through the jungle or continue to paddle and ride out the river. I thought: *What have I gotten my son and myself into?*

It's Okay to Ask for Help

Fortunately, the trip had several experienced river guides from the states who had come to Costa Rica to experience whitewater rafting during the winter in the states. The river rapids were good from their perspective, and the water was 30ºF warmer than back home.

In my life on land, I had learned to ask for help if I was afraid or stuck. So, if I could swallow my pride, this was no different. *Why not check out my fear to see how to manage it more effectively?* My idea was that experienced river guides had probably dealt with a rafter's fear before, so I would ask them for their ideas on how I might better tackle my fear.

The first river guide shared that, in his experience, some people became fearful after being tossed out of the raft and began projecting on the upcoming rapids. In their mind, they would stack one rapid on top of another. This means that they envisioned one huge rapid to go over rather than going over each rapid separately. His suggestion to me was: *Take one rapid at a time.* This made sense, so I relaxed and talked with the second river guide.

The second river guide listened to my question. He thought: *People would be pretty safe if they followed the safety rules,* such as not trying to stand up in the river and remembering to float down the river feet first. His experience was that more people injured themselves playing volleyball, badminton, or catch at the camp than river rafting. The key concern for not standing up in the river is to avoid getting a foot lodged between the rocks and the water's force bending you over and breaking your leg or causing you to drown.

I also found the third river guide's comment very useful: *You're here to have fun and play. Yes, there is a risk of going into the river, but that's the fun of it. Trying not to be tossed out of the raft is the game, but being tossed into the river isn't so bad.* He suggested that when the river was smooth, I jump off the raft and enjoy the river. Feel the warmth of the water. Play a little in the water so it wouldn't feel so strange or fearful when I'm tossed out going through the rapids—and there was a pretty good chance that I might be again.

I thought that was an interesting perspective. Here I was, afraid of water, something I had been very comfortable with since I was a competitive swimmer at the University of Minnesota. What I was fearful of was being dumped out of the raft going through a rapid and putting my life at risk. There was always the possibility of my hitting rocks, but I did have a helmet, and there were always safety kayakers around to pull me out if I did get ejected.

So, on this trip, I learned three great lessons on how to deal with fear:

1. Take one rapid at a time.
2. Follow the safety rules.
3. Relax and have fun.

My Approach to Deal With Fear Today

When considering situations in which I'm struggling with fear, I find it helpful to review all my lessons:

1. I'm *always at choice*.
2. It's okay to ask for help.
3. Be an observer of the observer I am—assess which beliefs hinder me and which help me.

How am I looking at my situation? What happens if I change my view?

1. Be aware of *False Expectations Appearing Real.*
2. Take one rapid at a time.
3. It's essential to break the experience into stages I can handle.
4. Follow the safety guidelines.
5. Remember to have fun and enjoy the experience.
6. Keep breathing.
7. If I follow the rules, I'll be safe.
8. There are always people I can ask for help, and they will help me.

For You to Consider

What huge fear have you created by adding all the barriers together?

What huge fear can you address by listing all the barriers and obstacles, then selecting and dealing with the most important ones?

How can you get yourself unstuck to take the necessary action and have fun creating the desired result?

Who can you call on to help you if you're still uncertain about how to proceed or if you should falter for some reason?

CHAPTER TWELVE

Let Horses Be Your Guide

There are several therapeutic methods with horses by many names.

The therapies I'm most familiar with are:

- Equine Gestalt Coaching Method
- Equine-Guided Coaching
- Equine-Assisted Psychotherapy

The Equine Gestalt Coaching Method helps clients become aware of their emotional blockages and unfinished business that may be holding them back. My favorite therapy is Equine-Guided Coaching. I've personally experienced breakthroughs in dealing with some of my other losses and issues. In workshops I've led with horses, I've experienced many people's significant breakthroughs. There is something special about the horse showing up in their authentic listening mode that stimulates healing communication. If you're angry, the horse will give you feedback. If you're hurting and need love, the horse will be there for you.

When I first started working as a business development specialist, there were two primary areas I focused on:

1. Helping people understand what they want to create in their lives and businesses.
2. Helping people take the necessary actions to create the desired results.

By applying the creative problem-solving facilitation techniques I'd learned, I realized I had a gift to help people and their business teams clarify what they wanted to create. Still, many people needed help to implement their goals.

I tried my selling skills—but they didn't work to move people past their stuck area.

I tried consulting and providing advice. That didn't work, either.

That's when I began my search for a better way to help people move past the stuck areas that were holding them back. I decided to learn about personal coaching. At the time, *coaching* was a new term in the market. When I told people I was a coach, they immediately thought I was an athletic coach. Working with horses to help people have breakthroughs was even lesser known.

At this point, I had studied Ontological Coaching at The Newfield Network for two years and had attended several international ontological conferences in Chile. After my Newfield experience, I had studied Somatic Coaching at the Strozzi Institute for more than two years. In one of those sessions, I was exposed to Equine-Guided Coaching (EGC), facilitated by Ariana Strozzi Mazzuchi. This personalized coaching method utilized the horse's ability to always be present, and it raised my self-awareness about how I was showing up as a leader. The session also helped me get in touch with some deep pain and shame that I was finally able to begin working through.

From that experience, I also learned how important it was for me to be centered when I made a request. Like Ariana said, "The cowboys didn't gallop all the way to the West Coast, they walked also." The lesson for me was to not always demand hyper-performance but to recognize that walking was a legitimate pace also. This awareness made me a better strategic planner and performance coach.

Horses live in the present moment and are highly tuned to our feelings. They read our human bodies on several levels of energy. They are sensitive to our sadness and anger and require us to be 100 percent committed when we make a request for them to move.

A Different Kind of Horse Sense

Some people feel they have experienced the spirit of a horse because they have ridden horses or grown up around horses. However, knowing horses in this way is much different from experiencing EGC.

At the beginning of my work with horses for personal growth, I had images of horses that many of us have, casting the horse in the role of working on a ranch with a herd of cows; pulling a wagon, a carriage, a stagecoach, or a plow; riding on trails; running at racetracks; performing in rodeos, dressage, or competitive show jumping but not working in the human development realm.

In my learning journey, I was fortunate to meet one of the great centered riding trainers, Mary Fenton. She said, "The art of centered riding is more about teaching the human than the horse. If the person learns to be calm and centered, they will have a better connection with the horse." EGC is extending this thinking to personal coaching and action.

Another interaction with horses is through therapy. Horse therapy encourages people to rebuild trust and boundaries in personal relationships and promotes adopting new problem-solving approaches.

Using horses to help people get in touch with and move through their blocked areas has taken off like wildfire in the United States and Europe. After becoming aware of the breakthroughs happening for people and my personal experience with EGC, I chose to study various approaches and practitioners earnestly. I secured my Bachelor of Arts in Architecture at fifty-five and began working on my master's degree in Equine Coaching. I embarked on a research study for my master's degree, which took me to workshops in California, South Dakota, Pennsylvania, Colorado, and Germany.

Honest, Frank Feedback for Personal Development
In my research, I found many examples of the benefits people were experiencing through equine-guided coaching and therapy.

Just a few of the people who benefit from some form of EGC are:

- *Sufferers of Post-Traumatic Stress Disorder (PTSD).* EGC methods are being successfully applied to the healing of war veterans, victims of violent crimes, and other sufferers of PTSD.

- *Survivors of sexual abuse.* Many sexual abuse survivors have credited Equine Gestalt Coaching for assisting them in healing the emotional scars of their pasts.

- *At-risk youth.* EGC methods are now widely known to turn lives around for At-Risk Youth. Consistent use of the work with horses has helped countless adolescents develop the confidence, calm, and focus necessary to avoid a life of gangs, crime, and incarceration.

- *Medical providers improving their sensitivity to patients.* Dr. Beverly Kane of Stanford University uses EGC methods to raise providers' awareness and sensitivity to the patient, improving the quality of care and lowering the number of malpractice lawsuits.

- *Children with autism.* EGC methods are employed as therapy for children on the autism spectrum, helping them develop emotional bonds, cognitive and language skills, and overcoming sensory disorders.

- *First graders learning about friendships.* EGC methods have been employed to help children recognize and appreciate the differences among people by recognizing the differences among horses. Through exposure to horses, children can become aware of incidents of prejudice among humans and learn about choosing a life of acceptance and tolerance.

A practitioner and teacher of EGC, Melissa Pearce does her work through her company called Touched by a Horse. Melissa's approach to the Equine Gestalt Coaching Method struck a chord with me. I highly recommend her certification program if you want to do gestalt work with horses.

I have witnessed Equine-Guided Coaches helping people, including me, through major stuck areas of their lives to develop essential leadership and teamwork skills.

EGC helped me overcome obstacles. Without it, I would not be doing what I am doing today. One session stimulated me to deal with an old emotional wound and complete my degree.

Additional Learnings from Equine-Guided Coaching
All my work with horses has been on the ground—no horseback riding. Grooming and leading are compelling learning experiences. I've experienced how coming from centered energy in my body and making requests of the horse to walk, trot, and canter can help me work more effectively with people. You might call it *developing leadership presence*.

One coach asked me to think negative thoughts when leading a horse. Within two to three minutes, the horse's ears turned to the angry mode, facing backward. It is a good lesson for how our thinking can affect our moods and conversations and the people around us.

I can recall many of my EGC experiences visually and emotionally because the somatic lessons are experiences locked in my body and mind and are available for recollection at any time I choose to bring them up.

A client's comment after one of my equine-guided coaching sessions resulted in my business name, "Stepping Through the Gate."

After her session, she shared these thoughts with me:

I always wanted to get into another field where I knew I would be more fulfilled, but for some reason, I could never get past the gate. You've empowered me to step through the gate to get to the other side and have a more fulfilling and satisfied life.

If you've found yourself stuck, blocked, or dealing with some deep emotional issues, I highly recommend investigating Equine-Guided Coaching or Equine Gestalt Coaching. I believe you'll be delighted with the experience and the results.

CHAPTER THIRTEEN

My Life Is Like a Garden Hose

One day, while driving with my daughter, Shelly, to put on a life-planning workshop with horses, I had an epiphany. Thinking about the barn and how we care for horses, I realized my life is like a garden hose.

You may think this is a strange comparison but let me explain.

Part of my development to become an Equine Guided Coach was to overcome my fear of horses. I volunteered to water and feed horses on weekends for the opportunity to lead the horses back from the paddock to their stalls. Before bringing the horses in, one of the tasks was to take the garden hose to the horse's stall and fill up the water bucket inside.

In a barn, there are generally two places to turn on the water—one at the hydrant where the hose was attached. The second is the nozzle at the end of the hose you put into the bucket hanging in the horse stall.

So, let me draw the comparison. Water is a life force we can't live without for humans and horses. Most of the time on a ranch or a farm, the water comes from a well.

First, the water source—our life force—is in the ground. We don't make the water; we tap into it. We can turn it on at the hydrant or with a faucet. We can open the hydrant or faucet fully or let the water gently dribble through the hose. We're at choice.

That's like the choices we make in our lives.

We can live our lives full of energy and fully engaged or let our life force dribble out and live at partial power. We have a choice.

This comparison gets even more interesting when you compare the size of the hose. The hose could be a garden hose, a fire hose, or a soaker. The hose's diameter affects how much water it delivers and how quickly. Like the choice of hose sizes, we can choose how fast we want our life force to flow in how we live. We can live as a garden hose at full strength, a fire hose at half power, or a soaker at just a dribble. The water pressure is available either way. We get to choose which way we want to live.

The end of the hose could also have a garden hose nozzle sprayer. The sprayer end of the hose is another place where we can control the water flow, our life force flow.

The water pressure is available within the hose. All we have to do is release it. Our life force is within our bodies; all we have to do is let it out. Our life is like the hose pressure; we turn the nozzle on to get as much water or energy as we want. Our option is to turn the sprayer and let out a little pressure if we only wish to have a dribble or open it and let it deliver water at full blast. The waterpower potential is always there. We're at a choice in what speed we want to live.

But the comparison doesn't stop there. Remember, as a kid, how you crimped the hose so the water would come through slowly enough so you could take a drink? Well, that's like your life. Sometimes, we crimp our life force with limiting belief systems. We can shrink our energy to a dribble depending on how we think when stuck or blocked. Open the crimp, and the full force of water can come through. Same with your life. Open the stuck, crimped areas, and your energy can return in full force.

And the analogy doesn't stop there. Several times, when watering horses in Minnesota during the winter, the weather got so cold that the water in the hose froze up inside the hose, and the hose had a big ice plug in it. The only way to get the water to the horses was to thaw the hose so the water would flow through it again.

So it is with our life. Sometimes our anger, resentments, and resignations freeze our life energy force. So, we must thaw it out with forgiveness, acceptance, love, and letting go to get the energy force flowing again.

Sometimes, hoses get cut, and the water or life force flows out of the garden hose at the wrong spot. So, we turn the water off at the hydrant to stop the water flow. This action enables us to repair the cut area or leak. Once we fix the hose, the water or life force can come through again.

It's like stopping and taking a break to get our life force flowing again after we've been knocked down by illness, the loss of a loved one, a divorce, a job loss, or a business shutting down or merging. When knocked down, we can turn off the hydrant until we repair the hose or our life and then open it up again once we improved the injured area. If we haven't fixed the hose correctly, another leak can spring. But if we've restored the hose well, it can be as good as new.

We're at a choice regarding how fully we want to live our lives. As a garden hose, a fire hose, or a soaker hose at full or restricted force.

We can choose whether to limit our energy from the water source—the hydrant, our higher power—or how we meter the water through a nozzle at the end of the hose.

We can decide if we want a temporary crimp to get a drink or stop the flow to repair the injured area. Things happen in our lives, and we must shut down and restore our life force flow.

Sometimes, we're just plugged up and need to thaw out to let the energy flow.

Thinking of our life as a garden hose with steady, sustainable water pressure is an exciting vision to make living easier.

CHAPTER FOURTEEN

Reduce the Impact of Your Judge and Saboteurs

I thought I was abreast of the positive and inspirational personal development concepts.

Even though I'd heard about Positive Intelligence® before, I'd devalued it as *New Age thinking*. I didn't explore it in detail until recently, and I didn't realize it was based on recent research on positive psychology, cognitive behavior psychology, neuroscience, and performance science.

I've been very impressed with what I've learned about Positive Intelligence® from Shirzad Chamine and Bill Carmody and with the possibilities that have opened for me and others by applying these new ideas and techniques.

My Foundation in Personal Development

As I've stated before, I've been using personal development ideas since I was twenty-seven years old, when I was introduced to *Psycho-Cybernetics* in a Toastmasters meeting.

From that book, I learned principles regarding the conscious and subconscious mind, the importance of having goals, and the choice between positive and negative thinking and visualization.

Maxwell Maltz's concept has been beneficial to me. I've used it for many years, and so have many trainers and coaches who work with athletes and clients to improve their performance and quality of life. For me, as good as *Psycho-Cybernetics* was, however, it never entirely addressed how to change some of my core negative mindsets that have dogged me all my life—like: *I'm not good enough, I'm not doing it right, I'm not adequate, I can't do that, That's not possible for me.*

Nor did *Psycho-Cybernetics* give me an approach to reduce the impact of these negative thoughts on my performance.

The Story of Two Wolves

The Story of Two Wolves is a good old story, and it comes in several versions, each with a big message. Here's the story that I like best.

It's about a man teaching his grandson about life.

"A fight is going on inside me," he told the boy. "It is a terrible fight, and it is between two wolves. One wolf is evil: He is anger, envy, sorrow, regret, greed, arrogance, self-pity, guilt, resentment, inferiority, lies, false pride, superiority, and ego. The other wolf is good: He is joy, peace, love, hope, serenity, humility, kindness, benevolence, empathy, generosity, truth, compassion, and faith. The same fight is happening inside you and every other person too."

The grandson thought about it for a minute and then asked his grandfather, "Which wolf will win?"

The old man replied, "The one you feed the most."

Again, a reinforcement for the idea that what you think about you will become.

Introduction of Positive Intelligence˚

In 2012, Shirzad Chamine, a coach and chairman of CTI, self-described as the largest coach-training organization in the world, published the book *Positive Intelligence˚: Why Only 20% of Teams and Individuals Achieve Their True Potential and How You Can Achieve Yours.*

Shirzad believes that when the mind is being positive, it flourishes. As a result of his research, Shirzad believes Positive Intelligence˚ is a significant factor in allowing us to reach our full potential. Moreover, his success stories back up his thinking.

Shirzad shares compelling reasons for focusing on, measuring, and improving our positivity.

Training the Mind

I didn't know it was possible to train my mind. Shirzad points out that Positive Intelligence˚ is based on the latest research in positive psychology, cognitive behavior psychology, neuroscience, and performance science.

The research identifies that core factors are at the root of optimal performance and mental well-being. Shirzad breaks our thinking into two approaches: Saboteurs and Sages.

Our Saboteurs cause stress, anxiety, self-doubt, frustration, regret, shame, guilt, and unhappiness. Suppose our mind regularly keeps us worrying at night, making us anxious about what we must do and judging ourselves and others' performance. In that case, Shirzad labels these ways of negative thinking as *Saboteurs.*

A *Positive Intelligence* *Quotient* (PQ*) is used as a measure of mental fitness. It's the percentage of time the mind is positive and allowed to flourish—a significant factor in enabling us to reach our full potential.

Overall Concepts of Positive Intelligence* include:

- Your mind is your best friend, but it is also your worst enemy.
- Positive Intelligence* is the relative strength of the two modes of your mind.
- A high Positive Intelligence* means your mind is your friend far more than your enemy; the low Positive Intelligence* is the reverse.
- Positive Intelligence* indicates how much control you have over your mind and how well your mind acts in your best interest.
- And, wonderfully, *positivity* is a skill you can build by flexing the correct muscles of your mind.

The primary Saboteurs identified in the research include ten archetypes:

- Judge
- Controller
- Avoider
- Victim
- Stickler
- Pleaser
- Restless
- Hyper-Rational
- Hyper-Achiever
- Hyper-Vigilant

Shirzad introduces two regions of the brain serving the Sage and the Saboteur. The region of our brain that the Sage lives in handles challenges in ways that produce positive emotions, such as curiosity, empathy, creativity, calm, and clear-headed, laser-focused action.

"Through Sage thinking, we perform better and feel happier," he says.

The Judge, which exists in all of us, finds faults with self, others, and circumstances. It causes much of our disappointment, anger, regret, guilt, shame, and anxiety and activates other saboteurs.

My Saboteurs were generally in this ranked order when I did my Saboteur Assessment:

1. *The Hyper-Achiever*, dependent on consistent performance and achievement for self-respect and self-validation. Highly focused on external success, leading to unsustainable workaholic tendencies and loss of touch with deeper emotional and relationship needs. For the Hyper-Achiever, self-validation, self-acceptance, and self-love are all conditioned on continual performance. This is often the result of either conditional or altogether absent validation from parental figures. Even with very loving and approving parents, it is easy for children to get the sense that they are loved in return for achieving, obeying the rules, having good manners, and so on, rather than unconditionally. This explanation fits very well with my childhood experience of starting school early and dealing with the challenges of my mother's illness.

2. *The Avoider*, focused on the positive and pleasant in a powerful way. Avoids difficult and unpleasant tasks and conflicts.

3. *The Pleaser*, needs to be liked by people and attempts to earn being liked by helping, pleasing, rescuing, or flattering others. The Pleaser needs frequent reassurance from others about their acceptance and affection. The Pleaser can't express their own needs openly and directly. They do so indirectly by having people feel obligated to reciprocate care.

4. *The Controller*, anxiety-based. Needs to take charge and to control situations and people's actions to one's own will—high anxiety and impatience when that is not possible.

5. *The Stickler*, perfectionist with a need for extreme order and organization.

6. *The Hyper-Rational*, focused intensely and exclusively on the rational processing of everything, including relationships. They can be perceived as cold, distant, and intellectually arrogant.

7. *The Hyper-Vigilant*, characterized as having continuous intense anxiety about all the dangers and what could go wrong. The vigilance that can never rest.

8. *The Victim*, emotional and temperamental as a way to gain attention and affection. An extreme focus on internal feelings, particularly painful ones. Martyr streak.

9. *The Restless*, constantly searching for more incredible excitement in the next activity or constant busy-ness. Rarely at peace or content with the current activity.

Positive Intelligence Determines Your Potential

What I like about Shirzad's information is that it puts science on our side to help us be winners in the game of life.

I recall his saying, perhaps in a lecture, something like:

> When our mind is on our side, we *flourish*. When our mind works against us, we *flounder*:
> Our potential is determined by many factors, including our cognitive intelligence (IQ), our emotional intelligence (EQ), and our skills, knowledge, experience, and social network.

Research with over 500,000 participants has shown that "PQ˚ is the best predictor of how happy we are and how well we perform relative to our potential."

According to Shirzad, the great news is that we can improve our PQ˚ significantly in as little as twenty-one days. With higher PQ˚, teams and professionals ranging from leaders to salespeople perform 30–35 percent better on average. They also report being far happier and less stressed.

Since I've started doing PQ˚ Reps, I've found myself being calmer when addressing challenging situations. The stress and the anxiety of performance have been reduced.

These statistics were impressive to me. I hope they are for you also.

I encourage you to take a closer look at creating a Positive Intelligence˚ practice for improved performance and well-being.

My suggestion as a place to begin:

1. Look at the website: www.positiveintelligence.com.
2. Take the Saboteur survey.
3. Listen to the audiobook or purchase the book.
4. Do the PQ˚ practices.

CHAPTER FIFTEEN

Clear Intention With Intense Implementation = Success

I didn't start as a strategic planning facilitator or life transformation coach. In fact, it all happened because I was capitalizing on my gifts, my talents, and my clients' needs. Initially, my planning skills revealed themselves when I was a sales representative for 3M Company in Milwaukee, Wisconsin.

I had a significant marketing problem to solve. I had a machine to sell in Madison, Wisconsin, and I wasn't doing well. So I designed what I now realize was a marketing plan. I wrote it up and sent it to the Division Marketing Department in St. Paul, Minnesota.

I called the event "The Eye Opener." To make the plan work, I first had to sell the machine to a dealer and promise to help them sell the machine to a printer. Then, I had to develop plans for tracking appointments and contact information for prospective customers. I wanted to include a live demonstration, so I invited someone with a printing press to be part of the demonstration.

The results of the mini trade show were excellent. We sold the machine off the floor. Every machine that went into Madison in the next five years was to someone who attended the first Eye Opener. The Division Marketing department sent out my plan to the rest of the country for sales representatives to use with their dealers.

Later in Milwaukee, I used a similar technique to sell an art product to graphic artists. Then I planned another Eye Opener event for Appleton, Wisconsin, with a third dealer, and we sold two machines off the floor.

When I got promoted to 3M marketing, I took a meeting management skills course, which taught an innovative way to solve problems using the wisdom of the group. The process was called *Synectics*. It is a marvelous process. It uses the collective wisdom of the group to create solutions for a specially defined problem.

The combination of my natural talents to see patterns while I facilitated solving the problem and my expanded knowledge of planning helped me succeed in my strategic planning consultancy business.

Here's what I learned about strategic planning. It's not just about business goals and market trends. It's about aligning your plans with your personal values—those core beliefs that guide your decisions and actions.

Six Approaches to Planning

I discovered there are six basic approaches people use to plan:

1. *Chaos.* People spend their time working "in" the business versus "on" the business, as they chase after crises in a reactive mode.

2. *Visualization (Speculation)*. This process uses visualization to see the goal or target for success and imagine what is necessary to arrive there.

3. *S.W.O.T Analysis (Strengths, Weaknesses, Opportunities, Threats)*. Assessing what resources are available, what strengths to capitalize on, what weaknesses or pitfalls to avoid, identifying which opportunities to pursue and threats to avoid. Working proactively to make the most of the current situation.

4. *Intense Analysis*. Analysis is beneficial, but when this approach receives too much attention, I've found from experience it can lead to *analysis paralysis*, and progress is inhibited.

5. *"Biz Plan" Software*. Software that offers a step-by-step plan for a bank or investment group to follow is available; however, I've found that these plans aren't very helpful as implementation plans.

6. *Four-Phase Strategic Planning Process*. This process takes the planner through four phases with the final phase being an implementation plan that includes clear measurements of success. This process is covered in more detail below.

In my opinion, the strategist Peter Johnson defines strategic planning well, so I've adopted his definition:

Strategic Planning is a comprehensive, highly organized approach on how to work smarter rather than harder by:
Doing the right things
At the right time
For the right reasons

I believe that success is the sum of clear intentions combined with intense implementation. This philosophy has worked for both my life and the business plans I've helped companies create.

I've since learned how important it is to be aware of the *observer I am*, a concept that refers to our individual perspectives and how they influence our actions. I now understand that because of this phenomenon, there's a possibility that I could take intense action to create the results, focus on solving the wrong problem, and not create the intended results. In other words, you could take a lot of action, but if you don't define the problem correctly, you won't get the results you want.

To avoid those pitfalls and to keep myself in check, I developed the Four-Phase business planning process to help me focus:

- *Phase One:* Situation Analysis – here is where we look closely at the business, answering questions related to all elements of the business—the customers, services or products, market potential, sales distribution, pricing, competition, and so forth—and the problems and opportunities in each category.
- *Phase Two:* Strategic Overview – This phase assesses and prioritizes the issues, opportunities, and metrics of success.

- *Phase Three*: Strategic Objectives – This phase builds consensus regarding the vision, mission and goals. It is complete with action plans for each of the goals and identifies the conditions of satisfaction.
- *Phase Four*: Intense Implementation – This phase is 75 percent of the planning and plan implementation process. Action plans with target dates are regularly reviewed. If the desired results aren't achieved, adjustments are made to correct the problem.

I've used this four-phase planning process for over thirty years to guide myself and others. In my experience of facilitating multiple planning sessions across various businesses, I've learned five critical things:

1. Clarity of focus is essential to success; however, it is only 25–30 percent of the effort. I believe a good plan, poorly implemented, is more successful than a vague or generic plan implemented with brilliant precision. Gaining clarity regarding what you want to accomplish is critical for achieving the desired results.

2. Nothing happens without intense implementation, and implementation is 70–75 percent of the planning effort. But remember, a lot of plans get written yet aren't regularly reviewed. When a business I was working with was in trouble, I would encourage them to review their progress every two weeks. When the leadership team performed well in accomplishing

their goals, we reviewed their progress monthly. This regular review is your compass, keeping you on track and in control.

3. The leadership team could create good results if we focused on the 20 percent that made the difference, a concept known as *Big Rocks First*. It's desirable to have no more than five key goals, which are the big rocks that should be prioritized in planning and execution.

4. Not everyone on the Leadership Team had the mindset to take action. Some people were blocked or stuck with limiting beliefs. Initially, I'd try to sell the new idea to the management team. Then I'd try to give them advice, which was only listened to some of the time. Once I realized we were limited by our beliefs, I started learning about coaching—a much more effective process of helping people get unstuck.

5. It's essential to learn *Linguistic Acts*, a term that refers to the use of language to create actions and results (see Chapter Six for a thorough explanation). Learning to be accountable, to make explicit requests, and to effectively manage promises are critical for building trust and getting the desired results in the business.

My Three-Phase Life Planning Process
I discovered the core business planning principles I was using also applied to life planning with only a few modifications. It's

critical to develop a clear focus and to intensely implement what you declare you want to achieve. This is when the real transformation happens, when your intentions turn into tangible results, and when you feel the power of your actions shaping your life.

I use a three-phase planning process to clarify my life focus for the upcoming years:

1. *Phase One.* I review my accomplishments for the previous year. I am specific in documenting my results. The concept is to leverage what I do well and to improve on what I could have done better, if it is needed, to achieve my goals.

2. *Phase Two.* Develop an assessment of where I am in my life—at that moment. One of the best assessment tools I've found is the Fully Effective Executive Assessment, taken from the book *The Fully Effective Executive* (McGraw-Hill Contemporary, 1983) by Gerald Kushel. Every year, I rated myself and considered what steps I might take to improve my scores. I determined my progress and identified the key areas I needed to focus on the following year.

3. *Phase Three.* I clarified what I wanted to create in the upcoming year and which areas to focus on. After Shirley's death, I realized my priorities changed. Raising and supporting my children in their life journey became more important than seeing how much income I could earn or what level in corporate management I could achieve. I started with Personal Wishes. Then, I would develop a list of the categories vital to me. I set goals, strategies, and action plans to implement the following year.

I kept annual goals to a critical five: I'd found that having six or seven key goals was too hard for me to manage and track, and it dissipated my energy. Getting my core tasks done with more than five goals was challenging, so all areas suffered.

This discipline also worked for the businesses I coached. I choose to focus on the 20 percent that makes 80 percent of the difference. Intensely implementing core goals impacted my achievements substantially.

My Typical Plan Outline:

- Determine what I wish/intend to create.
  - My Declarations *(things I had the authority to create)*
  - My Core Values
  - My Measurements of Success
- Nonfinancial
- Financial
- Determine the Natural Gifts and Talents I want to capitalize this year.
- Decide on My Driving Force. (My Super Goal).
  - Live my life with Joy, Peace, and Serenity
  - Remember I'm *always at choice*
  - Remember I'm accountable and responsible for what I create
  - Be an Observer of the Observer I Am
  - Ask for help where needed
  - Build Trust by making explicit Requests and managing Promises

CHAPTER SIXTEEN

How to Establish Priorities – Matched Pairs

It's been my experience that most people have difficulty prioritizing more than five items. I've found this Sort and Stack process to be one of the best for prioritizing many items. It enables me to quickly focus on the 20 percent that makes 80 percent of the difference. See if it makes a difference for you.

Sort and Stack **Prioritization Process**

1. *Get the ideas onto paper.* If you don't have a written list, take a few moments to write down the key things you want to accomplish. Learning to set priorities becomes much easier when people shift to focusing on the Big Rocks first. Big Rocks are the 20 percent of the effort that makes 80 percent of the difference in moving your projects and life forward.

The questions are:
- a.   What *are* the big rocks?
- b.   What *is* the 20 percent?
- c.   How *do* I find these Big Rocks on my to-do list?

2.   *Sort.* Take your long list of things to do and sort them by priority level: High, Medium, and Low.

For each item on the list, ask yourself: *What do I hope to accomplish with my project? Business? Life? How important is accomplishing this particular task or project?*

You should be able to work through this process relatively quickly. Don't belabor the decision for each item; go with your first instinct.

When you finish your Sort, you will have three lists:
- a.   High-priority items
- b.   Medium-priority items
- c.   Low-priority items

Set the Medium and Low-priority lists aside for now.

When working with a long list of items, do not skip the Sort!

I once assigned a client the task of prioritizing her values. Unfortunately, she didn't know how to sort a long list of values into High, Medium, and Low categories, and I didn't tell her. She ended up with the lengthy and mind-numbing task of doing matched pairs with seventy items! Sorting into High, Medium, and Low categories and focusing on the high-priority items are essential to working with a manageable list.

3. *Stack.* Working with the high-priority items from your sort, you will now stack them and rank them in priority order using the powerful matched-pairs method. Let's say you have a list of five High-priority, nonsorted items in front of you:

> Item 1
> Item 2
> Item 3
> Item 4
> Item 5

Start by comparing Item 1 against Item 2. Ask yourself: *Which one of these items is more important to accomplish? Which item will have the more significant impact in moving my project and life forward?*

If Item 1 is more important than Item 2, place a slash mark next to Item 1 so that your list looks like this:

> Item 1 /
> Item 2
> Item 3
> Item 4
> Item 5

If the opposite is true, place a slash mark next to Item 2 instead.

Now repeat, working your way down the entire list, comparing Item 1 to Items 3, 4, and 5, one at a time, placing a slash mark next to the item of greater importance each time.

4. Now, go back and start sorting the list by comparing Item 2, one at a time, to the remaining 3 items (compare Item 2 against Items 3, 4, 5).

    After you finish with Item 2, repeat, comparing Item 3 to the remaining two items, and so on, until you have gone through all the items. When you finish, your list may look something like this:
    Item 1 /
    Item 2 / / / /
    Item 3 / /
    Item 4 / / /
    Item 5

5. Finally, stack the items in your list according to how many slash marks each received, from the most to least. In our example:
    Item 2 / / / /
    Item 4 / / /
    Item 3 / /
    Item 1 /
    Item 5

    You now have a prioritized list of your Big Rocks—a ranked list of the 20 percent effort you need to make 80 percent of the difference in completing your project or living your life purposefully. Begin by tackling the top item in your stack (Item 2 in our example), and you're off and running.

Applications of the Sort and Stack Method

There is no limit to how this powerful and straightforward prioritization process can be applied. I've seen this process used for planning vacations (e.g., What sites are must-sees for our group?), family decisions (How should we spend our family fun time today?), business planning (Which activities deserve our attention for business development?), life planning (What values are most important to me?), and measurements of success (What elements help me assess my success?).

In every case, more achievements will be desired than are possible to complete. Using the Sort and Stack process is like saying, "I recognize that I may not be able to get everything done, but if I get these key things done, I will be happy." The matched pair process keeps you focused on the most essential items rather than thinking everything is—or should be— possible.

Equally as important, the matched pair process gets you out of limbo (inaction) and bypasses the trap of focusing on the little things that don't make much difference.

Some checking questions:

- What is the most challenging action item on your to-do list?
- Do you have a clear set of prioritized action items to help you move your project or life forward?
- How will using the Sort and Stack method help you focus on the 20 percent that makes 80 percent of the difference?

My Recommendations

I've benefited from annual planning and so have the businesses I've coached. If you're self-employed or want to advance within a corporation, I encourage you to do life planning beyond just financial planning.

I recommend that you use an excellent annual assessment tool. The one that worked best for me was from Kushels's book, *The Fully Effective Executive*.

Get clear about your gifts and talents that you want to capitalize on.

Get clear about your Core Values.

Select the five key things you want to accomplish in the upcoming year—establish strategies and action steps with timetables.

Regularly review your progress—monthly, quarterly, annually.

Here are a few final thoughts I want to share with you regarding planning.

- It's simple—it's just not easy
- Live fascinated about the possibilities instead of in fear of the unknown
- Enjoy the journey.
- Make sure you have fun! Life is too short not to.

CHAPTER SEVENTEEN

Zigzag to Success: Learning From Failure and Mistakes

Thank you for joining me on my learning journey, which has involved making mistakes, failing, and learning from the experiences.

By tracking my learning journey, I hope you realize you are *always at choice*, and your life is full of choices.

The first choice I strongly suggest you consider is being a lifelong learner. It was not my original intention to be a lifelong learner after college. I never thought it a possibility. But from experience, I've learned that this approach to living has kept me curious about life and its possibilities. My commitment to lifelong learning has kept me fully engaged in my *gifted years*—the years beyond eighty.

I warn you: Lifelong learning is not without its struggles. If you're committed to being a lifelong learner, you're guaranteed to experience a lot of time as a beginner in the initial steps of learning something new. My experience is that as a beginner, I make more mistakes and fail often. I used to get down on myself when I was learning something new. If I made mistakes, I felt like a failure. I know if I look upon my mistakes as failures and can't do the tasks, I can easily zoom off course. Now, I look upon my mistakes as a beginner in learning a new thing; I'm just unable to do it correctly *yet*. In my beginner learning stage, I can ask what I can do better next time. I call this process *zigzagging to success* by learning from my mistakes and failures. It just means I have yet to succeed and have more to learn.

One thing to remember: It's almost impossible to go from being a Master in one domain of learning to being Competent in another domain of learning without starting off as a Beginner.

The Stages of Learning I apply are:

- Master/Teacher
- Expert
- Proficient
- Competent
- Novice
- Beginner
- Unconsciously Incompetent

We're *always at choice* regarding how we look at a situation. One way is to view the situation as The Judge would, as a negative. The other option is to look at the situation as an *opportunity*, a *gift*. We can see the opportunity from the perspective of a supportive, wise Sage.

One thing we all can agree on: Life is not a dress rehearsal. There are no do-overs. The full scope of human life is relatively short. Life is short, even if we live to be 110.

We've all experienced some lives that are shorter than others. There are no guarantees. We will spend much of our time learning how to live, and then we will pass on.

One crucial question to ask ourselves:
How much time do I have left?
Followed by: *Am I using it wisely?*

One way to look at life is to compare it to a river. The river, as life, keeps flowing. Sometimes, the river floods and destroys things in its path that must be rebuilt. Sometimes rivers become rapids; some are just little ripples we can easily float over, and some are life-threatening class IV and V rapids. After a strong rapid, there is generally an eddy—a circular current of water, a small whirlpool. Sometimes, things get stuck in the eddy. When that happens to people, they can have difficulty getting out of the whirlpool without help. Learning to ask for help is extremely useful when we're in an eddy in our life.

Living our lives wisely is a choice. For some, living a life of leisure is wise for them. Living in a community with lots of fun activities and chances for learning is another opportunity.

For some, living wisely means taking trips to experience other areas and cultures.

For others, it's spending time with family.

What's fulfilling to me is being of service. The research supports that if we live our lives with a purpose, we will likely extend our lives by seven to eight years and be fulfilled and appreciated in the experience.

It's important to remember that we only have one opportunity to live. We choose how we want to live and what we want to create. We can also decide how we want to measure our success.

It's helpful to remember that we're *always at choice*. Even the choice of not making a choice is a choice.

It took me a while on my life journey to realize that I wanted to create a life filled with Joy, Peace, and Serenity. It's incredible how that choice made such a difference in my life.

I also chose to be a lifelong learner. This choice isn't for everyone, but it has added a lot to my life. Being eighty-six and learning how to write and become a published author has been an exciting, engaging, and challenging experience for me.

In my learning journey, someone once told me that experience was the best teacher, and I don't always have to learn from my own experience. I did learn from others' experiences. Hopefully, what I've shared has given you new insights into how to look at your life and access to some marvelous teachers.

Best wishes for an incredible life journey.

Blessings,

Larry

Transformation Tools

During my learning journey, I came across several transformation tools that have been extremely helpful during challenging times. Many of these tools I would read in my darkest days and reflect on them to change my mood.

The Serenity Prayer

The "Serenity Prayer" from Alcoholics Anonymous was a good way to ground myself when things around me were chaotic. "The wisdom to know the difference" puts the responsibility on me, the reader.

The short version of the prayer:
God, grant me the serenity to accept the things I cannot change,
The courage to change the things I can,
and the wisdom to know the difference.

And the full version of the prayer:
God, grant me the serenity to accept the things I cannot change,
Courage to change the things I can,
And wisdom to know the difference.
Living one day at a time,
Enjoying one moment at a time,
Accepting hardships as the pathway to peace,

Taking, as He did, this sinful world
As it is, not as I would have it,
Trusting that He will make things right
If I surrender to His Will
So that I may be reasonably happy in this life
And supremely happy with Him
Forever and ever in the next.
Amen.

I'm in Need Of . . . Of What?

"I am in Need of . . . of What?" has been my favorite poem-prayer to read during my traumatic times. It appears in *Guerillas of Grace: Prayers for the Battle*, by Ted Loder.

Well, God, I made it through another sweet-sour time
and here I am,
>   nibbled,
>   frazzled,
>   puzzled,
>   awed.
in need of . . . of what?
A chuckle, maybe,
>   a revolution begun with a belly laugh,
>   a Bronx cheer in the face of the onslaughts
>   of disaster and death itself.
Such is my need;
and this is my wonder:
>   Are you really as humorless,
>   as grimly serious
>   as I have made you out to be?

Or do aardvarks and monkeys,
    bullfrogs and platypuses,
        puppies and porpoises,
           and people, perhaps,
  reveal the comic side of your grace,
    the playful side of your love?
Tickle me into giggling down
  the wailing walls
    of my endless grievances.
and trip up my waddling pomposities.
Lord of laughter, as of tears,
shake me awake
and teach me to laugh at myself,
  at my black-draped solemnity,
     over my petty preoccupation with success and
       failure,
         through all the hurt and adversity
until my laughter lures me deep
  beneath the terrors without names,
    beneath the questions without answers,
      beneath the pain without relief;
lures me deep
  to the love in me unused,
    to the strength unspent,
      to the courage untapped,
        to the dream unrisked,
          to the beauty unexpressed;

all the way down
   to the inescapable bottom,
      to the awareness that I must get on
         with being who I am
           as fully as I can,
              as unflinchingly as I can,
                 as accurately as I can,

which is to say,
   as gracefully,
      as powerfully,
         as faithfully
as you have created me to be.

Autobiography in Five Short Chapters

"Autobiography in Five Short Chapters," accurately reflects my stages of growth. I found this poem by Portia Nelson when I attended Adult Children of Alcoholics.

I

I walk down the street.
There is a deep hole in the sidewalk.
I fall in.
I am lost.
I am helpless.
It isn't my fault.
It takes me forever to find a way out.

II

I walk down the same street.
There is a deep hole in the sidewalk.
I pretend I don't see it
I fall in again.
I can't believe I am in the same place.
But it isn't my fault.
It still takes a long time to get out.

III

I walk down the same street.
There is a deep hole in the sidewalk.
I see it is there.
I still fall in.
It's a habit.
My eyes are open.

I know where I am.
It is *my* fault.
I get out immediately.

IV
I walk down the same street.
There is a deep hole in the sidewalk.
I walk around it.

V
I walk down another street.

Big Rocks First

This story from an unknown source will remind us to put things into perspective:

One day an expert on the subject of time management was speaking to a group of business students and, to drive home a point, used an illustration those students would never forget.

The man stood in front of those high-powered overachievers and said, "Okay, time for a quiz." Then he pulled out a one gallon, wide-mouthed mason jar and set it on a table in front of him. He produced about a dozen fist-sized rocks and carefully placed them, one at a time, into the jar. When the jar was filled to the top and no more rocks would fit inside, he asked, "Is this jar full?"

Everyone in the class said, "Yes."

Then he said, "Really?"

He reached under the table and pulled out a bucket of gravel. He dumped some gravel in and shook the jar, causing pieces of gravel to work themselves down into the spaces between the big rocks. He smiled and asked the group once more, "Is the jar full?"

By this time the class was onto him. "Probably not," one of them answered.

"Good!" he replied.

He reached under the table and brought out a bucket of sand. He dumped the sand in, and it went into all the spaces left between the rocks and the gravel. Once more he asked the question, "Is the jar full?"

"No!" the class shouted.

Once again, he said, "Good!"

Then he grabbed a pitcher of water and began to pour it in until the jar was filled to the brim. He looked up at the class and asked, "What is the point of this illustration?"

One eager beaver raised their hand and said, "The point is, no matter how full your schedule is, if you try really hard, you can always fit some more things into it."

"No," the speaker replied, "that's not the point. What this illustration teaches us is: If you don't put the big rocks in first, you'll never get them in at all."

After reading this story, what do you consider to be the *big rocks* in your life? Time with your loved ones, your faith, education, finances; a specific cause; teaching or mentoring others; a project that *you* want to accomplish?

Remember to put these big rocks in first, or you'll never get them in at all.

Take a minute to reflect each morning and ask yourself this question: *What are the big rocks in my life?* Then, put those in your jar first.

Wisdom

Here's another great story from an unknown source that puts the American way in perspective and stimulates the question: Why do we strive so hard to make money?

An American investment banker was at the pier of a small coastal Mexican village when a small boat with just one fisherman docked. Inside the small boat were several large yellowfin tuna. The American complimented the Mexican on the quality of his fish and asked how long it took to catch them.

The Mexican replied "only a little while."

"Then why didn't you stay out longer and catch more fish?" the American asked.

I have enough to support my family's immediate needs."

"But what do you do with the rest of your time?"

"I sleep late, fish a little, play with my children, take siesta with my wife, Maria, stroll into the village each evening where I sip wine and play guitar with my amigos, I have a full and busy life," the fisherman replied.

The American scoffed. "I am a Harvard MBA and could help you. You should spend more time fishing, and with the proceeds, buy a bigger boat. With the proceeds from the bigger boat, you could buy several boats, and eventually, you would have a fleet of fishing boats.

"Instead of selling your catch to a middleman, you would sell directly to the processor, eventually opening your own cannery. You would control the product, processing and distribution. You would need to leave this small coastal fishing village and move to Mexico City, then LA, and eventually NYC, where you will run your expanding enterprise."

"But, how long will this all take?" asked the fisherman.

"Fifteen to twenty years."

"But what then?"

The American laughed and said, "That's the best part. When the time is right, you would announce an IPO and sell your company stock to the public and become very rich, you would make millions."

"Millions. Then what?"

The American said, "Then you would retire. Move to a small coastal fishing village where you would sleep late, fish a little, play with your kids, take siesta with your wife, stroll to the village in the evenings where you could sip wine and play your guitar with your amigos."

Resources

BOOKS

<u>Personal Development</u>

The 7 Habits of Highly Effective People: Powerful Lessons in Personal Change. Stephen R. Covey. Simon and Schuster (30th anniv. edition), 2020.

The Anatomy of Change: A Way to Move Through Life's Transitions. Richard Strozzi-Heckler. North Atlantic Books, 1997.

Change or Die: Could You Change When Change Matters Most? Alan Deutschman. Collins, 2007.

Choicemaking: For Co-Dependents, Adult Children and Spirituality Seekers. Sharon Wegscheider-Cruse. HCI, 1986.

Do the Work: Overcome Resistance and Get Out of Your Own Way. Steven Pressfield. Black Irish Entertainment, LLC; 2015.

Life's Greatest Lessons: 20 Things That Matter. Hal Urban. Touchstone, 2003.

Meeting Jesus Again for the First Time: The Historical Jesus & The Heart of Contemporary Faith. Marcus J. Borg. HarperOne, 1995.

The Missing Piece. Shel Silverstein. HarperCollins, 1976. A simple and touchingly told fable that gently probes the nature of quest and fulfillment.

Please Understand Me: Character & Temperament Types. David Keirsey, Marilyn Bates. Prometheus Nemesis Book Company, Inc., 1978.

Psycho-Cybernetics: A New Way to Get More Living Out of Life. Maxwell Maltz. Simon and Schuster, 1960.

The War of Art: Break Through the Blocks and Win Your Inner Creative Battles. Steven Pressfield. Black Irish Entertainment, LLC; 2012.

Where Do I Go From Here With My Life? A Very Systematic, Practical, and Effective Life/Work Planning Manual for Students of All Ages, Instructions, Counselors, Career Seekers, and Career Changers. John C. Crystal and Richard N. Bolles. Ten Speed Press, 1982. *(Out of Print)*

Who Moved My Cheese? Spenser Johnson. Putnam Adult, 1998.

Finding Purpose

"The Philosophy of Ikigai: 3 Examples About Finding Purpose." Jeffrey Gaines. Scientifically reviewed by Maike Neuhaus. 17 Nov 2020. positivepsychology.com/ikigai

The Power of Purpose: To Grow and to Give for Life. Richard F. Leider, David A. Shapiro. Berrett-Koehler Publishers (4th edition), 2025.

Dealing with Grief and Loss

Transitions: Making Sense of Life's Changes, Strategies for Coping With the Difficult, Painful, and Confusing Times in Your Life. William Bridges. De Capo Lifelong Books, 2004.

The Way of Transition: Embracing Life's Most Difficult Moments. William Bridges. De Capo Lifelong Books, 2001.

Effective Conversations

Conversations for Action and Collected Essays: Instilling a Culture of Commitment in Working Relationships. Fernando Flores, Maria Fores Letelier, Ed. CreateSpace Independent Publishing Platform, 2013.

You Are What You Say: The Proven Program That Uses the Power of Language to Combat Stress, Anger, and Depression. Mathew Budd and Larry Rothstein. Harmony, 2001.

Business Development

The Discipline of Market Leaders: Choose Your Customers, Narrow Your Focus, Dominate Your Market. Michael Treacy and Fred Wiersema. Basic Books, 2007.

Customer Intimacy: Pick Your Partners, Shape Your Culture, Win Together. Fred Wiersema. Knowledge Exchange, 1996.

Leadership Development

The 21 Irrefutable Laws of Leadership: Follow Them and People Will Follow You. John C. Maxwell. Thomas Nelson Publishers, 1998.

Developing the Leaders Around You: How to Help Others Reach Their Full Potential. John C. Maxwell. Harper Collins Leadership, 1995. eBook.

Developing the Leader Within You: Workbook. John C. Maxwell. HarperChristian Resources, 2000. eBook.

Failing Forward: Turning Mistakes Into Stepping Stones for Success. John C. Maxwell. Harper Collins Leadership, 2000. eBook.

The Leadership Dojo: Building Your Foundation as an Exemplary Leader. Richard Strozzi-Heckler. Frog Books, 2007.

The Oz Principle: Getting Results Through Individual and Organizational Accountability. Roger Conners, Tom Smith, and Craig Hickman. Portfolio, 1998.

The Wisdom of Oz: Using Personal Accountability to Succeed in Everything You Do. Roger Conners and Tom Smith. Portfolio, 2016.

Working Ourselves to Death: The High Cost of Workaholism and the Rewards of Recovery. Diane Fassel. iUniverse, 2000.

TRANSFORMATION POEMS

"Autobiography in Five Short Chapters." *There's a Hole in My Sidewalk: The Romance of Self-Discovery.* Portia Nelson. Simon and Schuster, 1993. I found this poem when I attended Adult Children of Alcoholics. I felt it accurately reflected my stages of growth.

"I'm In Need of . . . of What?" *Guerillas of Grace: Prayers for the Battle.* Ted Loder. Fortress, 1981.

"Wild Geese." *Wild Geese: Selected Poems.* Mary Oliver. Bloodaxe, 2004.

COACHING TRAINING AND WORKSHOPS

Foundations of Ontological Learning Coach Training. Coaching for Personal and Professional Mastery, Newfield Network North America Headquarters: Denver, Colorado. (303) 449-6117. connect@newfieldnetwork.com. newfieldnetwork. com

Onsite Workshops: Living Centered Workshop. Sharon Wegscheider-Cruse and Joe Cruse, original founders. Onsite is an emotional-wellness healing facility dedicated to changing the world through enhanced emotional health. For over forty years, Onsite has offered world-renowned emotional wellness retreats, therapeutic intensives, residential trauma care, and digital resources. 1044 Old, Hwy 48 N, Cumberland Furnace, TN 37051 (615) 789-6609. experienceonsite.com

Somatic Coach Certification Program, "The Art of Somatic Coaching." Strozzi Somatics and Embodied Learning Methodology. Richard Strozzi-Heckler, senior teacher and advisor; Staci K. Haines, senior teacher and co-designer of methodology and teacher training. Strozzi Institute for Somatics, 6 Strong Place, Brooklyn, NY 11231. courses@strozziinstitute.org. Text or call: (302) 428-9397 or (510) 853-9559. strozziinstitute.org

EQUINE COACHING WORKSHOPS

Leadership & Horses™, SkyHorse Academy. Ariana Mazzucchi, founder, somatic coach. Casari Ranch, Santa Rosa, California. 707-338-9817. SkyHorseStaff@gmail.com. arianamazzucchi@gmail.com. www.CasariRanch.com

Touched by a Horse Equine Gestalt Coaching Certification Program. Melisa Pearce, teacher, author, psychotherapist, Gestalt therapist, and pioneer in the field of the human/horse healing. 5350 Taylor Renee Circle, Elizabeth, CO 80107. (303) 440-7125._office@touchedbyahorse.com. touchedbyahorse.com

HELPFUL PERSPECTIVE TOOLS

Center Yourself: A One Minute Meditation. Dr. Gerald Kushel, author of *Fully Effective Executive.* This is a simple way to center oneself before going into an important meeting.

"What *Does* It Mean to Be Successful?" Hal Urban. *Life's Greatest Lessons: 20 Things That Matter.* (Simon & Schuster, 2005). 6–7. These ideas of what it means to be successful changed my perception of how to look at my life and the contribution I was making.

Acknowledgments

This book could never have been completed without the love and support of my four wonderful children. They all earned college degrees from the schools of their choice and supported me in my own learning after their mother passed away, helping me become a better father.

My two wives: Shirley Troff, the wonderful birth mother of our four children, and Dodie Driscoll, who wholeheartedly embraced my children and became the wind beneath my wings, enabling me to succeed in my profession. My children adored her. Unfortunately, she passed away before this book was published.

I want to thank all the fabulous teachers I've learned from. I've listed many of them in my resource list. I apologize to all the wonderful teachers I haven't acknowledged, especially the horses who shared their wisdom with me in the equine coaching sessions.

I'd also like to thank the Seshat Press Team for the outstanding writing and publishing support I received from Carrie Jareed, Christine Kloser, Karen Burton, Penny Legg, Ellen Monsees, Jean Merrill, and especially my editor Heather Taylor, who refined my manuscript, clarified my thoughts, and made my book much easier to read and more useful for my readers.

I feel fortunate to have had opportunities to see and experience the world rich with blessings. I'm grateful for the opportunity to be on this earth for this brief time. I hope my thoughts have helped you move forward with greater joy, satisfaction, and fulfillment in your lives.

March 30, 2025

Contact Larry Freeborg

Can I Help?

I am a life transformational coach and the founder of Stepping Through the Gate. My unique gift is helping individuals move through major losses and trauma in their lives to become fully engaged in their new life possibilities.

I provide one-on-one transformation coaching to help you move through your loss of a loved one. I also offer presentations on "Always at Choice" and "Be the Observer of the Observer You Are".

If after reviewing my services, you would like to explore how I can help you deal with your challenges and achieve what you hope for, please email me and arrange for a complementary phone consultation.

Our discussion will help you become clearer about what you want to achieve and where you're stuck. I'll help you identify what's holding you back and we can discuss how to "unlatch" the beliefs to achieve the results you desire.

I look forward to speaking with you.

Larry Freeborg
www.alwaysatchoice.net
freeborg.larry@gmail.com

Testimonial

I always wanted to get into another field where I knew I would be more fulfilled, but for some reason, I could never get past the gate. You've empowered me to step through the gate to get to the other side and have a more fulfilling and satisfied life.

—An Equine-Guided Coaching Client
(Their comment led to the business name "Stepping Through the Gate.")

About the Author

Larry Freeborg is an eighty-six-year-old, deeply experienced life transformation coach who helps people struggling with losing a loved one and trauma.

In addition, he's a strategic planning facilitator who works with individuals and privately owned businesses, helping them create fulfilling, enjoyable lives and successful, profitable companies.

His personal experience of losing his wife Shirley to leukemia when she was thirty-nine years old and instantly becoming a widower with four young children to raise and losing a job in a suffering economy shaped the foundation of his thirty-year coaching and facilitation practice.

To support his clients in achieving their goals, he has blended his life transformation with vast experiential learning to help others move through their personal loss, grief, and stuck areas to achieve their goals.

He is the founder of Stepping Through the Gate and works from his home in Chippewa Falls, Wisconsin, on Lake Wissota.

Larry grew up in St. Paul, Minnesota, went to Murray High School, and graduated from the University of Minnesota with a degree in Architectural Design at age fifty-five. He has raised four lovely children and spent the second part of his life with his lovely life partner, Dodie.

Prior to publishing this book, Larry lost his second wife Dodie to a falling accident. She was eighty-one years old. He was able to use many of the lessons he learned dealing with the loss of Shirley to deal with the trauma, deep grief, sense of loss, and life refocus much easier than before.

Different than his experience with Shirley's death and four young children, Larry's close adult family have come to his aid with deep caring, love and support. Dodie was a blessing to them also.